HEBREW ASTROLOGY

HEBREW ASTROLOGY

The Key to the Study of Prophecy

By

SEPHARIAL

Author of
"The New Manual of Astrology," "The Dictionary of Astrology," "Transits and Planetary Periods," "The Solar Epoch," "Science and Foreknowledge," "The Daily Guide," "Astrological Ready-Reckoner," etc.

PHILADELPHIA
DAVID McKAY COMPANY
WASHINGTON SQUARE

CONTENTS

HEBREW ASTROLOGY

INTRODUCTION

In these days of advanced thinking it is a matter of common observation that we have left many of the old landmarks behind and that we are now pressing forward to greater heights and to a wider horizon than that which represented the mind-content of our progenitors. It has been suggested that human progress moves in cycles, and that we are continually reverting to the state of affairs and the theoretical outlook upon life that held the minds of former generations. The further suggestion is that we do not trace the same circle on the same plane, but that each successive return to our former condition finds us somewhat higher in the scale of civilisation and mental development. In fine, we are travelling by gradual ascent around a helix or spiral, so that our progress is always upwards but not always onwards. On the contrary it would appear to be backwards. This theory brings to mind the lines of Elizabeth Barrett Browning:

> " And does the path wind uphill all the way?
> Yea, to the very end."

At the same time it suggests that we might profitably acquaint ourselves with the inwardness of that intriguing work : " Civilization, its Cause and Cure," by one of our modern fresh-air thinkers, Edward Carpenter. Reduced to its real value, modern civilisation offers us small compensation for the amount of living capital that we put into it. Its rateable value is wholly fictitious. The constituents of good living are few and simple, which, when satisfied, leave us with immeasurable powers for mental and spiritual progress and adequate time in which to employ those powers. But the present high and artificial standard of living leaves little enough of either power, time or inclination for self-development. Consequently we have to learn as we go, and all our information has to be so presented that " he who runs may read." We have become a race of paragraph readers and précis writers. The bulk of the population of the world has also become parasitic and opportunist ; always following closely upon the food-line, with eyes lowered to the search, they seek ever to reap where they have not sown, to prey upon the faculty of others, to take profit from another man's labour. It is quite suitable in this place to ask whether after all the game is worth the candle ? It does not appear that we are nearer to either God or Nature than our progenitors, or that we get more out of life that is of permanent value to us than they, if indeed as much.

I am forced to this frame of mind by the consideration that in ages past there were men who attained to the great height of direct communion with God, who were able to receive His word and inspiration and had power given them to carry out His behests. They were enabled to study the laws of Nature and to perceive in them the imprint of the Eternal Mind. They were aware that Life throbbed with a rhythm that was the very heart-beat of the earth on which they lived. They scanned the heavens and set the bounds of the seasons, they watched the moving worlds among the steadfast stars, and saw that at the root of all this pageantry of the midnight skies there lay an eternal purpose, the purpose of God. That purpose meant a plan. They studied to understand this plan of the Divine unfoldment in human life, and they came by inspiration upon the knowledge of the cyclic law. The eyes of faith penetrated into the mists of futurity and the evidence of the unseen lay open before them. They saw a world created for a purpose, a great racial selection made for a purpose, and a plan which provided against all contingencies forever

working out to its fulfilment. Consider what
may be the full meaning of life to such as these :
" Abraham, my friend," " Jacob whom I have
blessed," " David whom I have anointed," and
" My Son, in whom I am well pleased," and when
it is remembered that all were, by natural descent,
Chaldeans, none with any depth of consciousness
can fail to see that these elect of God were under
no obligation to either the civilisation or the
" modernity " of their times for what they were
or the places they filled in the connected plan and
set purpose of God.

Modern science has discerned a law of periodicity in regard to natural phenomena, and almost
the first thing that is required by way of demonstration is the graph, whether of frequency or
energy, showing these features in the course of
their recurrence. The periodicity of sunspots,
for example, shows a return of maximum frequency after a period of 11.2 years, and though
no specific reason is advanced for this marked
periodicity, it is plainly enough demonstrated in
the chart or graph. It has been suggested that
the cause of electrical storms is the sunspot, but
it has not been officially noted that the same cause
that produces the sunspot may also produce the
storm. Sir Norman Lockyer sought to link up
the phenomena of sunspots with high and low

Nile tides, and later with droughts and floods. Similar investigations and suggestions have been advanced by others in regard to the periodicity of zymotic diseases, whether epidemic or endemic; which facts are brought forward in order to show that nature works by a species of pulsation, answering to a definite beat of time. In all there is an awareness of an underlying law of manifestation which appears to have escaped not detection but definition. It will continue to baffle the minds of men until they recognise that man is an integral part of the great universe of life about him, that he is compounded of cosmic elements, and touches his greater environment at all points. Neptune is our present limit of the solar system. Its existence was discovered from the observed perturbations of the nearer planet Uranus, which in turn was discovered by those of the planet Saturn. This was a double demonstration of the "solidarity of the solar system" so much talked about, but so little believed in, by our modern scientific exponents. But once the fact is demonstrated that nothing in this wide universe exists for and to itself alone, and that no part of the universe is so distant but that it is in immediate relations with every other part, it will be seen that man as terrestrial cannot escape the net of a material necessity. "The net of Heaven has wide meshes," says the Old Philosopher of China, " yet nothing escapes it."

When therefore we come to the consideration of this law of periodicity, we are brought into direct relations with these very bodies of our system which are the occasion of all periodicity whatsoever. Every single note in the octave produces its own set of vibrations which we call a note, and these vibrations produce their several sets of sense-impressions. When occurring in definite combinations they form chords, which give rise to a complex of impression which we call harmony or discord. It is even so in regard to the planetary *shemayim* or spheres, each of which has its own characteristic and place in the system. Indeed we cannot think of a " system " apart from this allocation of specific function in celestial economy attributable to each of the planets, nor can we think of a system as a co-relation of detached parts or organs, but only and always as a correlation of all the parts or organs, with their specific functions interacting one upon another. Even at the risk of being accused of respect for obsolete traditions, let us be logical in our use of words. And so long as the solar system coheres, this interaction of its planetary constituents will go on, merely waiting upon our recognition. The ancients understood better what little they are presumed to have known, than we whose vast overlay of encyclopedic knowledge may claim to understand any one of the multidinous facts which go to our modern learning. They looked upon Nature as a composite whole, nor did they set any bounds to the field of her operations. They had more than enough of evidence in support of the fact that Nature does not cease to exist where we cease to perceive her. They understood the limitation of the senses. They understood the limitless power of the Spirit.

The law of cyclic unfoldment may be regarded as the long swing of the pendulum of time. The Great Plan may be likened to the mainspring which depends for its continual flow of energy upon the winder. The flywheel, which in this sense corresponds with the law of periodicity, depends upon the escapement. As the flow of blood from the heart throughout the system is regulated by the arteries, so the energy of the mainspring is regulated in its release by the escapement. Periodicity is the recurrent manifestation of the cyclic law. The cyclic law is the expression of the Divine Plan.

Quite recently there has been considerable interest in seismology, due to the alarming frequency and violence of shocks in almost all parts of the globe. Theories galore have been formulated to account for these outbursts, but nobody has succeeded so far as to predict when these shocks would occur, except the author of the " Geodetic Theory " which recognises the fact of interplanetary action. In this the planets in their courses form parallels and conjunctions, oppositions and quadratures, the more significant being those formed by Mars with Neptune, and Uranus with Jupiter. The theory jumped into recognition by the prediction of a series of definite dates in the year 1923 when great disturbances of the earth might be expected, which duly came about, the stated dates being never more than 24 hours out one way or the other. Writing in 1925 about the forthcoming geodetic quadratures of four of the major planets, Mars, Neptune, Jupiter and Saturn in May 1926, it was said that " the indications were so unusual that something in the nature of a widespread series of earthquakes might be expected, the effects being very severe." In 1928, the subject again sprang into prominence owing to the devastations in Bulgaria and Greece, and notably at Philippopolis and Corinth, which were laid in ruins. The *Morning Post* acknowledged as received in March, the prediction of earthquakes on 3rd April and 22nd of the same month. On April

3rd five shocks were experienced at Smyrna. At Torbali in Angora strong shocks occurred on the same date, by which 1,543 houses were destroyed, out of a total number of 2,000 all told. Thus three-quarters of the township were destroyed. On that date there was no confirmation of shocks in the stated locality of Messina and Calabria but on the following day, 4th April, Rome reported insistent shocks in Carnia, at Cavazzo and Verzegni which started a landslide, masses of the mountain being detached, the church of San Floreano, a national monument, being seriously damaged, the high altar smashed and the tower in danger of falling. The mountain at Versegni was split for over a thousand feet, and great devastation of property followed. Three weeks later a further terrific series of destructive shocks were experienced in Corinth, the distress being such that the British Government thought well to send a relief flotilla of three cruisers to succour the impoverished and distracted victims. The possibility of prediction is therefore well attested and is eloquent in support of the ancient belief in interplanetary action. To them the man was mind, and the earth was body, and they knew by inevitable law of consequence resulting from the dependence of matter from the Spirit, that every change of mind induced concomitant physical effects, and that what was true of the man was true also of humanity. Terrestrial disasters were for them the consequent effects of either spiritual decadence, mental obliquity, or moral turpitude. We hardly need to seek deeper or wider for the causes of our multifarious troubles.

Out of this ancient belief in the interplay of planetary forces as affecting human life, there arose a complete system of Prognostic Astronomy which now goes by the name of Astrology. After some centuries of Egyptian and Greek usage the system became departmentalised and remains so at this date. Thus we have the Mundane, Genethliacal, Horary, and Geodetic departments of interpretation of planetary influence. Fundamentally they are the same, but a brief description of each will enable the reader to distinguish between them.

Mundane Astrology is directed to the prediction of the trend of events in the state or country for which the chart of the heavens is set. It extends to the prediction of outstanding events affecting the welfare of the country, the fiscal and commercial affairs of the people, the relations of the government and the people, and similar matters of public importance. In this connection the Ingresses of the Sun to the four cardinal signs of the zodiac, which are used to define the

Seasons, are employed, and the chart of the heavens for the moment of the sun's ingress is set for the longitude and latitude of the capital. Subsidiary indications are derived from the time of the lunations which occur within the limits of the Quarter of the year under consideration. In this system the significance of the signs of the zodiac occupied by the planets at the time, is of considerable importance, as each sign is held to have rule of specific countries, in confirmation of the statement that the Adamic heritage is divided into "twelve parts, according to the number of the Tribes of Israel." Very many remarkable correct forecasts have been made by even modern astrologers, and it is customary to refer to these vaticinations as " lucky shots," though most frequently the astronomical indications from which they were made have been cited. The odds against any political event being predicted correctly both as to time and nature, are many thousands to one. In any case it would seem that the astrologer is able at all times to give a coherent reason for the faith that is in him, which is more than can be said for many modern theorists.

Genethliacal Astrology is related to individual nativities, and seeks, through a knowledge of the nature and operation of the planets and signs

B

of the zodiac, to define the potentialities of a person. The physical constitution, health, characteristics, personal peculiarities or defects, financial prospects, position, occupation, marriage, progeny, friendships and alliances, etc., are usually dealt with. It is not presumed that this system of interpretation goes further than to define aptitude, potentiality, and opportunity for self-expression. It has been well said that character and environment make up destiny. This has been categorically confirmed by the verdict of Thackeray : " Sow an act and reap a habit ; sow a habit and reap a character ; sow a character and reap a destiny," with the omission of the all-important modifying factor of environment, which admittedly counts for so much of human action. For environment is a far-reaching influence. It embraces training, education, dietary, clime, association, and opportunity, without the favouring influences of which even the best faculty is apt to remain in obscurity. In this system of Genethliacal Astrology, a measure of time is employed which attests its ancient origin, namely, " a day for a year," which, it will be remembered, was the key to Scripture prophecy given to the people of Israel. " I have appointed unto you a day for a year, a year for a day. Behold, I have given it unto you," saith the Lord.

Proceeding on this basis, it is held that the state of the heavens for any number of days after birth will define the state of affairs with the individual at the same number of years. Hence arises a system of prognostic astronomy which has held the attention of dispassionate and unprejudiced minds by force of evidence from one generation to another throughout the ages.

Horary Astrology relies upon the sympathetic relations that continually exist between the heavens and man, and seeks thereby to interpret and define any issue that may arise in the mind. This is done by reference to a figure of the heavens set for the time at which any crisis occurs in the affairs of life. William Lilly, the friend of Sir Elias Ashmole and adviser of many illustrious men of his own day, was a past-master of this art. Owing to the ascendancy of the more rigid methods of mathematical astrology as applied to the doctrine of nativities, the use of Horary Astrology has greatly declined, it being held that what is not potential in the horoscope of birth cannot find eventuation in the course of daily life. Many students also regard this branch of the science, still very much in vogue among the Hindus and Arabs, as being in the nature of divination, and therefore incapable of scientific statement or systematic proof. Undoubtedly its virtue lies wholly with the individual faculty of the astrologer, whose knowledge of symbolism may not reach to a true statement of an issue. It is not the sort of Astrology that " instructed and compelled the unwilling belief " of such a man as Kepler or which held the mind of Tycho Brahe in profound respect of the science, nor is it at this day advanced by those who regard Astrology or rather *Astrologia sana* as entitled to a place among the sciences.

Geodetic Astrology is the more modern aspect of the science which has relation to the prediction of earthquakes, terrestrial phenomena, storms, etc., as affections of the body of the earth itself. It has assumed an instant importance from the fact that earthquakes have been accurately predicted, as well as floods and storms. In this system the scientific basis of Astrology is adhered to very rigidly, and the solidarity of the solar system is continually brought into evidence by reference to the geocentric positions of the major planets, i.e., their positions as seen from the centre of the earth. In this connection eclipses play an important part as premonitory indications of internal disturbance of the earth, the subsequent formation of definite angular positions of the planets on the line of the eclipse being stimulating factors which bring those indications into effect.

As some reference to this aspect of the subject has already been made in this Introduction, there is no need to elaborate at this point.

It is open to any person of average intelligence with the aid of an astronomical ephemeris reduced to geocentric equivalents from the Nautical Almanac, and any one of the recognised standard works on the subject of Astrology, to examine and prove the matter for himself. What is at all times most objectionable is that spirit of prejudice, allied to its twin giant, ignorance, which continually bar the way to all progress in this as in all other subjects of an empirical nature. It may be recalled that Mr. Halley of comet fame had the temerity to upbraid Newton for his belief in Astrology, and on that occasion received the only rebuke which, in the circumstances, seemed appropriate: " I have studied the subject, Mr. Halley, you have not." Chief among the critics of Astrology are those who confessedly have no knowledge whatsoever of the subject. Dr. Butler, Chaplain to James, Duke of Ormonde, had a prejudice against the subject and set out to write against it, but considered it due to his reputation as an intellectual man to first study the elements of the science. He concluded his work by writing a book wholly in defence of Astrology. Indeed, it is within the experience of the present writer, that no single person has ever essayed the dispassionate study of this ancient science without being wholly persuaded of its paramount truth.

At its base we find, in short, that Astrology affirms the unity of life, that it recognises the dynamic relations between the various bodies of the solar system, that it maintains the dependence of the terrestrial upon the celestial world, and affirms that the planets and luminaries are the divinely appointed agents for the distribution of all such influences as they may be held to exercise in the economy of the system to which they belong. Raised to its higher octave, Astrology affords us the only means of understanding the working out of the great law of cyclic unfoldment in human life and hence is the only key to prophetic interpretation. It shows the existence of law and order throughout the varied experience of life, and proves, as no other science can prove, that human agency is the means employed by God for the working out of His set purpose and plan in regard to humanity. In these pages it will be shown by what measure that plan has been adhered to in respect of a people elected and trained by Him to become the pioneers of the future humanity, how they have been into the melting-pot, under the hammer and over the grindstone, to the end that they may be His battle-axe, an effectual weapon against the tyrant and the oppressor, and the safeguard of His Commonwealths.

If, after reading this testimony, there remains any doubt in the mind as to the existence of this purpose and plan in regard to the world at large, the reader has but to study the subject from the point of view of the individual unit of life, apply the science of Astrology to his own case, and then reason with himself whether, if the unit is under tribute to the law, the mass can be said to be free of it. What may be called the mass-chord of a family is the aggregate of influence exerted by its units, and what we argue of a family extends to the nation, and to the race at large, so that in effect the integrity of any people depends on the recognition of that law which binds man to man and people to people in the common task of self-realisation and the enjoyment of that security and freedom which results from obedience to the law of Heaven. The revelation of this " law of Heaven " by the mouth of the prophets " which have been since the world began," puts us in the position of becoming divine conspirators towards the earlier and fuller realisation of that " one divine, far-off event, to which the whole creation moves," the realisation of God's Kingdom on earth.

CHAPTER I

CHALDEAN ASTRONOMY

THERE is no subject engaging the modern mind equal in interest to that aspect of Cosmic Symbolism which may be called the Science of Foreknowledge, and which popularly goes by the name of Astrology. No less an authority than Sir Isaac Newton has stated that Seth, the third son of Adam, was the founder of astronomy, its symbolism, and all that it may be held to signify.

Accepting the reputed date of the Adamic Epoch as —4000 the birth of Seth would fall in the year —3870. Up to the present time we have no authentic evidences of so high an antiquity of astronomical science, but we are able to say with perfect certainty that Alexander the Great took Babylon by the defeat of Darius III in the year —334, and that Callisthenes then presented to Alexander a complete record of the astronomical observations of the Babylonians, covering a period of nearly 1600 years, since they date from the year —2230. These records had reference to the rising and setting of the stars and planets in relation to the position of the sun; new moons, full moons and eclipses being recorded; and various celestial phenomena duly noted, all to the effect of showing a more or less complete knowledge of the motions of the planets and the mapping of the heavens into asterisms. They knew the length of the year and the value of a lunation and subdivided the zodiac into " signs " and " asterisms " in order to define the division of the year circle into twelve months, and the daily motion of the moon in relation to the sun.

According to the Shu King or Historical Classic of Confucius, the Chinese tradition is equally ancient and as fully developed. The ancients had both official Observers and Recorders who were responsible for public notices of all forthcoming eclipses, and for the due regulation of the Calendar and public Festivals. In common with the ancient Aryans they made use of a Sixty-year Cycle, a year of twelve months, and a lunation of 29 to 30 days.

In ancient Egypt there was a very exact knowledge of astronomy and although this appears to have been very largely if not entirely in sacerdotal custody, it is to this source that the great Hebrew legislator, Moses, owed his earlier education and training, for we are told that he was "learned in all the lore and language of the Egyptians." And some four centuries before his day Jacob and his sons were in full possession of the symbolism of the heavens, as revealed in the prophecies which emanated from that source.

Thus it will be seen that the study of the heavens is the most ancient form of exploration and scientific enquiry of which we have any record.

Latterly there has arisen fresh evidence of the marvellous precision of this ancient knowledge of the stars in the structure of the Great Pyramid, which until recent years has not been apprehended. It is now known that this great structure, the largest building of any sort in the whole world, was originally designed for the purpose, incidentally, of embodying the chief features of the solar system and principally the divisions of time effected by the relative motions of the sun, moon and earth. It is claimed that there is a prophecy by Isaiah which says that in the latter days of the Age there would be " a witness to the Lord of Hosts in the midst of the land of Egypt and on the borders thereof," and this prophecy appears to be fulfilled in the latter-day discovery of the cosmical intention of the Great Pyramid, for this structure lies at the head of the Delta just west of the Nile and on the thirtieth degree of latitude, so that it is " in the midst of the land " and inasmuch as it is situated on the 30th parallel of latitude, it exactly divides Upper and Lower Egypt, a division which is now official, but did not even exist in the days when the Pyramid was built.

The base of the Pyramid is four-square, its sides facing as nearly as possible due North, South, East and West. The length of one side of the base is 9,131 inches, and the four sides of the base thus measure together 36,524, which are the exact number of days in 100 tropical years. The sides of the Pyramid have a slope angle of 51° 52' and this gives a height of 5,813 inches. But 5,813 is the radius of a circle of 36,524, and thus again 100 tropical years are indicated as the centennial measure adopted by the builders, and this is found to be a most accurate value in the light of modern astronomical science. Not that the Pyramid as we know it to-day, distorted and disfigured as it is by the effects of vandalism, earthquake shock and attrition, answers precisely to these figures, but when restored to the original design—the inference of which is unescapeable —these values immediately appear. The marble casing stones have been removed, the base level has a definite subsidence towards one corner of its square area, and the whole structure has been moved fractionally out of the perfect line of orientation which it originally held. But by taking the mean length of the four base lines, with added casement stones, as 9,131 inches, equal to 100 tropical years in days, the rest of the features follow by mathematical consequence. Then it is found that the diagonal of the square base is 12,913 inches, and the sum of the two diagonals is therefore 25,827 inches, the exact number of years in the cycle of Equinoctial Precession.

In view of all these facts we may conclude without prejudice to our main argument, that the ancients were in possession of very considerable astronomical learning and we have now to show that to this astronomy they imported a Cosmic Symbolism which not only allowed of a prophetic interpretation, but was capable of application to mundane affairs in terms of human life and thought. In fine, they had no use for astronomy apart from its human application. Hence arose the whole science of Astrology.

ABRAHAM THE CHALDEAN

It is generally understood that astronomy had its birth in Chaldea. All Babylonian records would therefore be originally based on this source of information. To this wealth of knowledge the Patriarch of the Hebrew Race would have immediate access. The Chaldean tradition would doubtless be extended in every direction and would permeate the thought of many peoples, but the direct knowledge would be communicated in its integrity to the descendants of the Patriarch without doubt.

The average man regards all Hebrews as Jews, and there are some so woefully ignorant as to consider Abraham himself as a Jew. He was however a Chaldean by birth and emanated from the city of Ur according to the Biblical record in the year —1917. His son Isaac, and his grandson Jacob, were not Jews, neither were the sons of Jacob by name Reuben, Simeon and Levi. The fourth son of Jacob, born in the year —1753 was Judah, and his descendants were called Jews, an abbreviated and corrupt form of *Yahudim.*

Abraham, described as " Abraham, my friend," in the Word of God, doubtless held to the original concept regarding the nature and purpose of the stars of heaven. Having created the elements (*ath ha-shemayim, ve-ath ha-aretz*) of the heavens and the *earth,* the cosmical process of formation began and proceeded as set forth in the Genesis (Ch. I). The word *bra* (He created) is no longer used but the word *oshah* (He made) is brought into

the text to show that the Elohim employed existing elements in the building up process of the
cosmos or universe.   The idea that there can be
no light without the sun as a focal centre of
radiation shows ignorance of the nature of light-
production.   The use of electric light and radiant
heat ought to have long corrected this popular
misconception.   Therefore when it is said that
only in the fourth stage of cosmogenesis the
Elohim " made " the sun, moon and stars, it was
in relation to a pre-existent earth, already formed
by the same cosmic forces acting under and
expressing the Divine Intelligence.   These celestial bodies were to be not only for seasons and
days and years, and for the dividing of day and
night, but also for " signs " (*othuth*).   It is this
othic value of the celestial bodies that constitutes
the basic principle of Astrology, which, among
all the sciences has undergone least change in its
fundamentals and has persisted throughout the
ages.

Biblical references to the influence of the stars
in human affairs are not numerous but they are
explicit, and they may be regarded as carrying
weight only where there is an assurance of
authority in the Scriptures.   " The stars in their
courses fought against Sisera," conveys at all
events the express statement of belief in as-

tral influences by the writer of the Book of Judges (Ch. v, 20). But one need not seek higher authority for this belief than is given in the gospels, where, in reference to the signs of the end of the (*genea*) age or dispensation, our Lord expressly says: " There shall be signs in the heavens, the sun shall be darkened, the moon shall not give her light, and the powers of the heavens shall be shaken." The prevalent disbelief in any consummation of the age is well foretold by the apostle Timothy: " For now they say, Where are the signs of His coming ? for since the fathers fell asleep all things have continued as formerly until now." This question has its emphatic answer from the Science of Foreknowledge. The signs are in the heavens, exactly where they were foretold to appear, as will hereafter be fully revealed. In effect, then, the Chaldean tradition is seen to have persisted until this day as a principle of belief in planetary influence in human life, if not in the fulness of its original conception.

The Planets and Rulers

The science of the Chaldees as transmitted through Hebrew channels, adheres to the concept of the planetary bodies and the earth as being of the same nature, for when it is said that " God created the original matter (elements) of the heavens (ha-shemayim) and the earth," the word used for " heavens " is appropriately *shemayim*. This word is in the plural, and is frequently used to signify the heavenly bodies, and also states or planes of existence, extraneous and also superior to the earth, but there can be no doubt whatever that the root meaning of the word better suits the idea of *planets*, inasmuch as it signifies disposers, regulators, displacers or movers, which accords with the name planets, i.e., wanderers. That this is the intention of the Genesis account seems to be shown by the use of another word to indicate " stars " (*cochabim*) from the root *coah*, to burn. So that we may reasonably translate the text thus : " In the beginning the Elohim created the elements of the planets and the earth . . ." " And the Elohim made two great lights, the greater light for the rule of the day and the lesser light for the rule of the night, with the stars (*ve-cochabim*)."

The sevenfold male-female or positive-negative powers of the Creator are conveyed in the agglutined word Elohim (al-h-im) which from the root Al, a power, is here used in the male, female, plural form. This sevenfold power is concreted in the seven planetary bodies, which are held to be the collecting and distributing centres or rather agencies, through which the will of God is accomplished. The Seven Planets gave their names to the days of the week, and each of the planets was said to be ruled or presided over by an Intelligence, otherwise known as the Seven Lights, and the Seven Angels before the Throne. These were symbolically depicted in the Golden Candlestick with its seven branches.

THE SEVEN ARCHANGELS

The Seven great Lights or Intelligencies are variously named among the Kabalists, but the more generally accepted are :

MICHAEL, ruler of the Sun.

This name means literally : *Mi*, who ; *kah*, like; *el*, God, i.e., Who is like God, or perhaps, Who is like in power, and it may be an affirmation or an interrogation. It does most certainly convey the idea of a Supreme Intelligence, the greatest of the Lights before the Throne of the Ineffable.

GABRIEL, ruler of the Moon.

The word comes from *Geburah*, strength. It recalls the fact that grace and strength are from the same source, for the graciousness of the Eternal God is everywhere portrayed in the Word by the ministrations of the angel Gabriel.

C

MADIMIEL, ruler of Mars.

The word Mad denotes vehemence, zeal, ardour to the point of excess. Our equivalent word "mad" conveys a somewhat similar idea. The Maadim are represented in the nether sphere by those "vessels of wrath" whose principles are subversive of law and order and altogether destructive. They invest human forms but they are spirits of iniquity, and aptly described by the evangelist as "wandering stars."

RAPHAEL, ruler of Mercury.

This name comes from *raphah*, to heal. From this definition we derive immediately the symbol of the Caduceus, carried by the Greek god, Hermes (Mercurius). The Caduceus is probably a latinized form of the Hebrew *Kedeshi-ash*, i.e., Fire of the Holy Ones. As Merx, the planet Mercury is related to trade, hence merchant, mercantile, mercenary, etc., from the same root. Poetically Mercury is the winged messenger or sailing ship which is primarily responsible for the tradition of the nations of the earth.

ZEDEKIEL, ruler of Jupiter.

Zadok, holiness, justice, rectitude, righteousness. From this Spirit the judges of the earth are presumably drawn. Justice and equity are the essence of righteousness. The men who judged Israel, during three hundred and fifty-six years, from Joshua onwards to Samuel, were interpreters both of the civil and spiritual laws, their great prototype being Melchizedek (*Melech*-king, *zadok*-righteousness) King of Salem. He ruled in his own country and took tithes as a Priest from Abraham. Christ is called " a Priest after the Order of Melchizedek, without father and without mother, having neither beginning nor end of years," verily an embodiment of the Judge of all the earth.

HANIEL, the ruler of Venus.

From the root *hanah*, this name means the glory of God. The bright and morning star Venus is mystically referred to as Lucifer (*lux*, light ; *fero*, I carry) the Light-bearer, whose fall from heaven is associated with Hilel, another name for Venus, who as " son of the morning " represents the mystery of the incarnation of the sons of God or spiritual intelligences, which are collectively portrayed as Prometheus who taught men how to use the fire of the gods. In this light it is held to denote the Incarnation of the Son of God by whose descent into the world, liberation from Satanic thraldom is assured to many. In connection with this work of redemption, the Christ appears successively in the power of all the Archangels in whom is invested the power of God. Hence His ascriptions are many, but in relation to Venus He appears as the Prince of Peace.

ZOPHKIEL, the ruler of Saturn.

This name indicates the Mystery of God. It is related, through the usual designation of Saturn (Kronos) as the Father of Time, (or more familiarly "Father Time" with the hour-glass and sickle) with the Hebrew concept of the Deity as "the Ancient of Days" (*antiq-yomim*). The unfathomable mystery of the Eternal and the Infinite is guarded from mortal scrutiny and possibly from the questionings of even the denizens of the Spiritual World, by the Archangel Zophkiel, who arbitrates between Time and Eternity, and thus may be said to "measure the length of the measure of fate."

THE KABALA

WITHOUT an understanding of the Kabala or secret knowledge of the Hebrews, it would not be possible to go far in the task of unravelling these ancient mysteries, and a brief view of the principles of the Kabala will not therefore be out of place in a work of this sort.

Kabala means hidden or secret, whence we have our word Cabal for a secret conclave or council. Applied to the understanding and revelation of the inner meaning of Scripture, it may be accounted the Secret Doctrine or Esotericism of the Word. The chief work on the subject is the Zohar, the revelation or field of light. Many works have been written on the subject and several so-called expositions are more cryptic than the Kabala itself. What is known as the Tarot is an essential part of the Kabala. It consists of the Twenty-two Major Keys or laminae, the exempla of which were said to have been engraven on leaves of gold by Hermes the Thrice Great. These Keys are representative of steps in the work of Attainment. First there are the Ten steps of the Novitiate, then the Seven steps of the Adept, and lastly the Three steps of the Hierophant, ending in either 21, the Crown of the Magi, or 22 Madness.

The Kabala is divided into three main parts : 1 The Gematria, 2 The Notaricon and 3 The Temurah.

Gematria. Every letter of the Hebrew alphabet has a numerical value which follows the order of the alphabet from Aleph or 1, to Teth or 9. Then by Tens from Yod or 10 to Tzadde or 90, then by Hundreds from Qoph or 100 to Tau or

400. The values for five, six, seven, eight and nine hundreds are denoted by those letters which alter their forms when used as terminals, as for example, Caph 20, when used as terminal 500; Mem 40, when used as terminal 600. A name, word or sentence of the Scripture, when written in Hebrew, is transposed into figures or numbers. These are added together and constitute the numerical value of the same. The unit value of the same letters is then extracted, and it is then found that the inner meaning or Kabala of the name, word or sentence has a numerical value equal to the unit value thus extracted.

The Notaricon is a method of literal extension and combination. The letters of any significant word or name are taken as the initial letters of other words, and the text which answers to this in any other part of the Scripture is held to be the key to its interpretation. Similarly, the letters are taken from the beginnings and ends of the words of any pregnant sentence and are brought together to form new words which are explanatory of the sentence dealt with.

The Temurah consists of an exchange of letters according to set Tables called Tables of Tziruph, and the cryptic meaning of a sentence thus transmuted is resolved from the combination of letters thus derived.

In this connection a Kabala of considerable interest attaches to the number 153, which is the number of " great fishes " brought up in the net from the right side of the vessel. This answers to the prophetic words : " I will make you fishers of men," for these 153 are symbolical of the Elect. The number 153 is a multiple of 17 (seven plus ten) and so are the Greek values for the words " *to diktuon* " (the net) and " *ichthues* " (fishes). In the latter-day sector of the Great Pyramid time-circle, the first and last Low Passages, related to the Great War and the Great Tribulation, together amount in length to 153 inches. This double period makes of 153 twice that number or 306 and if this be multiplied by 17 which is the Key Number, the great fishes caught in the net, i.e., the Elect, we derive the product of 5202 (306 x 17) and this is exactly 100 times the length of the First Low Passages in inches. Then if the value 52.02 be multiplied by 30, the days in the mean month of the year-circle, we have 1,560 days, which was the exact number of days of the duration of the Great War, from 4th August 1914, to 11th November, 1918. Then for the Second and last Low Passage we have 153 less 52.02 or 100.98, half of which is 50.49 inches, giving 1515 days for the extent of the Tribulation.

Without a knowledge of the Hebrew text it is

impossible for the reader to understand any illustrations which might be adduced in connection with the three primary divisions of Kabala, and for this reason an example has been taken from the Greek, which is the more accessible text, and applied to the elucidation of two great latter-day prophecies : " There shall be wars " and " Then there shall be a great tribulation such as was not since the world began, nor ever shall be, and except those days be shortened there were left no flesh living on the earth, but for the Elect's sake those days shall be shortened."

CHAPTER II

TIME AND ITS MEASURES

FROM the dawn of human knowledge until to-day
there has never been any other time-sense than
that which is related to a cycle of 360 units. In
seeking for a unit of measure it was readily found
in the rotation of the earth on its axis, whereby
the sun was made to appear to rise, culminate,
set and rise again, so that from sunrise to sunrise
was accounted as one day. The first sunset and
the oncoming of night must have been a myste-
rious and awful phenomenon to the mature mind
of the primal ancestor. We who have gradually
become accustomed to the sight of the rising and
setting of the sun are not so impressed. For one
thing, we know the reason and occasion of it all.
Few people can remember when and where they
first saw the sun to set. But at whatsoever time
we may first become aware of the perception, we
are immensely impressed. We should be even
more so were we unable to account for it. But
to-day the facts are so well known and the
phenomenon so much a matter of routine expec-

tancy, that we do not speculate upon it. That the sun will rise to-morrow is a foregone conclusion and presumably will continue to be such until the crack of doom.

The day-circle was therefore the original of all other measures of time. It would not be long before Man discovered that after a period of 365 days the celestial and natural landmarks were the same, the courses of the stars, the succession of the seasons, these would aid him in his estimate of the true year length.

The tradition was that " in six days the Lord made the heavens and the earth." Six therefore became the working number and after a period of 60 cycles of 6 days, the circle of days would come to an end and begin all over again. So, whether the sun took more or less than this number to complete its circle of the heavens, it did not compass more than 360 degrees, which was the measure of the circle. But it was determined from the beginning that the number of days in the week was seven, and that each day was under the rule of one of the *shemayim* or planetary spheres. Therefore it was necessary to have a year-circle which was as nearly as possible an exact number of sevens. Fifty-one weeks would yield 357 days, but fifty-two weeks would yield 364 days and would simultaneously complete the fifty-second planetary cycle, so that by the addition of one day, making 365, the year-circle would be satisfied and the planetary cycle would be carried forward one step. Thus if the first year began with Sunday, after 52 weeks or 364 days, the next day or 365th would be Sunday again, and the next year would therefore begin on Monday. Thus after seven years the days of the week would repeat themselves, and this probably was the first cycle of time that the natural man had knowledge of. But at the end of seven years he would observe that he was nearly two days in advance of the sun among the stars, actually one day and three-quarters owing to the fact that the year is 365 and a quarter days, and seven quarters make one and three-quarters. At the end of 14 years this error would amount to three and a half days, and in 28 years it would amount to just one week. This was his opportunity to adjust the calendar. So at the end of the cycle of 28 years he put in an intercalary week and waited not for the sun to catch up with him. The solar year was therefore fixed and regarded as being 365.25 days in length.

But what would trouble him more than the sun was the speedy and changeful moon. He would see the new moon emerge as a finely cut crescent immediately after sunset on the evening of one day, and at sunset of the next day he would see the moon, now rather larger, some distance further east of the sun at its setting, and this would go on increasing day after day until at length on the fourteenth day the moon would not rise until the sun was setting, and then it would appear as full orbed. Day after day he would watch its decline, now gibbous instead of crescent, and would eventually see it engulphed in the rays of the morning sun. But after a brief interval of three or four days he would see it again as the crescent new moon. His count of days would be 29 or 30 from one new moon to the next. By closer observation he would soon determine the exact length of the lunation and might at first have been satisfied with an estimate of 29 and a half days. Beginning his months or moons from its first appearance at the New, he would find that at the end of twelve moons, there were still some ten or eleven days to come to the end of the sun-cycle or year. This enabled him to insert an extra month at the end of three years, and this intercalary month has been the practice among the Hebrews ever since the days of Eber.

Longer records of the passage of time would soon lead to the observation that at the end of every nineteen years the first New Moon of the year fell in exactly the same part of the heavens.

And so little by litle the astronomical knowledge of the ancients might have led to the precise regulation of times and seasons. But when one considers the slow progress of modern astronomical science from the days of Kepler to the present time, and the still slower progress that had place between Ptolemy and Kepler, we can readily understand that with no scientific means of observation at their disposal, advance was even slower in the remote ages of the world. Against this theory of the natural development of astronomical knowledge there loom up facts of the most tremendous significance. How many observers of the heavens have seen the planet Mercury with the naked eye? Yet this planet was one of the ancient Seven Lights and a very important one in respect of its reputed influence upon the human brain and nervous system, as appears from the collected works of Claudius Ptolemy, and later Arabian astrologers.

How were the days of the week so arranged that they run in decades according to the Chaldean order in such wise that the first of each decade gives its name to the day of the week? Who determined the well-known Chaldean order of the *shemayim?* Saturn, Jupiter, Mars, Sun, Venus, Mercury, Moon, from which order there is no departure throughout the ages until now.

Many years ago I showed that this order had respect to the apparent velocities of the several planets as seen from the earth, the nearest being the moon which had the greatest acceleration, the furthest being Saturn which had the least acceleration, the others being successively slower as they were distant from the earth. Observe that the ubiquitous Mercury has the greatest acceleration next to the moon, and the problem assumes considerable dimensions. But this is not by any means all that the adoption of the Chaldean order involves.

The Ancients had presumably no knowledge of the atomic weights of the superior metals. They, nevertheless, determined that the seven primary metals were ruled by the seven shemayim, gold by the Sun, silver by the moon, quicksilver by Mercury, copper by Venus, iron by Mars, tin by Jupiter, and lead by Saturn. Arrange the seven planets at the angles of a seven-pointed star inscribed in a circle, Saturn at the first angle, Mercury at the second, Sun at the third, Jupiter at the fourth, Moon at the fifth, Venus at the sixth, Mars at the seventh. Read in this order round the circle, they answer to the atomic weights

Saturn—lead—207
Mercury—quicksilver—200
Sun—gold—196

Jupiter—tin—118
Moon—silver—108
Venus—copper—63
Mars—iron—56

and having observed that this regular order of the atomic weights of the several metals is related to a certain order of the planetary bodies, proceed to count the planets alternately round the circle, and you find you have the order of the days of the week, thus :

Sun—Sunday
Moon—Monday
Mars—Tuesday
Mercury—Wednesday
Jupiter—Thursday
Venus—Friday
Saturn—Saturday.

And if this be deemed fortuitous or accidental, begin with the angle held by Saturn and trace the lines of the star, when it will be found that next to Saturn comes Jupiter, then Mars, then the Sun, next Venus, then Mercury and lastly the Moon, so that the Chaldean order emerges from apparent chaos to form the cosmos which is implied in the words, " and set them in the heavens." And since the Ancients did not make the atomic weights of the metals, even if they knew of them, it becomes a serious question as to how they were able to determine what planets ruled the several metals. In lack of any scientific statement on the subject, I am disposed to accept the ruling of Sir Isaac Newton, that the progenitors of our race were divinely instructed in all these knowledges. It would appear to be even so. We may conclude that there is a law of time-intervals which is subject to a geometrical and numerical expression in the same manner as are all other natural facts. Hence arises the well-defined " law of periodicity " familiar to modern science, and the greater law of time sequence known as the " law of cycles " or " the cyclic law," known only to students of the science of foreknowledge. The study of the cyclic law, more than all else, except the fulfilment of prophecy based on a knowledge of this law, serves to confirm the mind in the existence of a Divine Plan and purpose in the scheme of human unfoldment, testing, and election.

A Day for a Year

In Scripture we have reference to this law in several forms. There is a " time," which is a period of 360 days, the year circle. Mention is also made of " the dividing of time," and " seven times." These express definite periods when referred to the unit standard of measure. The simplest expression of this measure is " one day."

This in prophetic writing is equal to one year of 360 degrees or a period of 365.25 days. " A day for a year, a year for a day, behold I have given it you," saith the Lord.

In thus handing us the Key to the interpretation of prophetic periods God gave us the assurance that His Word may be tested and proved, and that it was open to the scrutiny of the understanding mind, with history as its progressively insistent witness.

Having established the value of the " time " unit as equal to 360 years, we are now able to apprehend the meaning of " seven times." This is 360 x 7 or 2,520 years, which is called a Prophetic Week. Half this is the " dividing of time " or 1,260 years, prophetically known as " a time, times and a half time " i.e., three and a half days or years, and as the latter, equal to " forty-two weeks." The " month of days " is one-twelfth of the year-circle of 360 and when used prophetically it means 30 years, a day for a year. We British who are of Hebrew origin and descent (*Brit*, a covenant) and (*Ish*, a man) from Abraham (Ibrahim), have a penchant for the duodenary system of notation, and despite all the allurements of the imperfect but ready system of decimal notation, we have kept to our ancient standards. The year is divided into 12 months, there are 12

D

hours of the day and 12 hours of the night on the clock-face, there are 12 pence to the shilling, and 12 inches to the foot. As will hereafter be shown, the inch is the unit of measure denoting a day, a month, or a year.

ANCIENT CYCLES

THE jointure of the sun and moon as chrono-crators or time-makers, gives rise to an important luni-solar cycle of 19 years, called the Metonic Cycle, after Meton its so-called discoverer. Thus from the year 1909 to 1928 is an interval of 19 years. There was a New Moon at the vernal equinox of March 21st in the year 1909, and consequently there was a New Moon on the same day of the year 1928.

Recently it has been discovered that a most perfect luni-solar cycle is contained in the period of 1,040 years, which I have referred to as " the implicit period " of Daniel the prophet. It is derived from the difference between the greatest and least of his explicit periods, namely 2,300 days and 1,260 days, which are prophetic years. In this period of 1,040 years there are exactly 12,863 lunations. Thus, the tropical year is 365.242264 days, and the lunation is 29.5305881 days according to the modern astronomical authorities whose figures are based on the most careful observations. The difference of 12,863 lunations and 1,040 tropical years is about one-four hundredth of a second of time. But from the consideration that Daniel existed long before Meton, it would appear that Palmoni, the wonderful Numberer, has justified the implication contained in the words : " Go thy way, Daniel, for the words of the book are closed up and sealed until the time of the end." In these days when even the " stones " are crying out, the findings of archæology and astronomy are confirming the Word. I have observed moreover that in the same period of 1,040 years there are exactly 13,903 revolutions of the moon in its orbit, each equal to 27.321 days. That there should be an exact number follows from the fact that there are an exact number of lunations, for if the sun and moon are conjoined on the equinox in any year, they will be together again at the same equinox after an interval of 1,040 years, and during this period there will be 12,863 conjunctions of the luminaries, while the moon will make 13,903 revolutions of its orbit, so that the three periods will end at one and the same moment of time. But it is, nevertheless, surprising to observe that the difference between 13,903 and 12,863 is just 1,040.

COMPARATIVE VALUES

THE comparison of the motions of the sun and moon, which are the primary time-makers, leads to some interesting results. The sun has a mean daily motion in the zodiac of 59′8″, and the moon 13°10′35″, so that the relative mean motions of the moon and sun are as 13.36827 to 1. Taken as degrees and reduced to minutes the value of 802.0962 is obtained, and this divided by 120 gives 6.68413 minutes of a degree. This is the daily motion of the apsis of the lunar orbit, i.e., the point at which the moon is either nearest to or furthest from the earth. And, in connection with this value of 120, which is one-third of the circle, it may be observed that when the sun and the moon are exactly one-third of the circle from their perigees, they appear as exactly of the same size.

These facts are not directly pertinent to the subject of prophetic cycles but they are directly confirmatory of the observation of the divine Plato, that "God geometrizes." And seeing that we are dealing with the time element in the matter of prophecy, it is of interest to observe the relations of the two great lights which respectively are responsible for the measure of the year and month.

The Prophetic Year

ALL circles that are concentric are equal to one another in regard to their circumferential divisions. Thus with the earth as the centre, we may describe around it the circle of the day, or the month, or the year, or any cycle of larger dimensions, and in all cases an equal division of one will be an equal division of all others. Thus one hour on the day-circle will be equal to an arc of 15 degrees, and two hours will be equal to 30 degrees, which is one month on the year-circle. The unit of measure is in all cases one degree or one three-hundred-and-sixtieth part of the circle. Later it will be shown that the unit of lineal measure is one inch, and that it is employed in the Great Pyramid to indicate one year, one month or one day.

At the rate of one circular year per day, the prophetic week of 2,520 years is found to be equal to the " seven days " of the formative work, miscalled Creation, and also equal to the " seven times " of prophetic dispensation.

The Working Number

THROUGHOUT the whole scheme of cyclic unfoldment the working number is six. This number squared is 36, the number of inches in the

British yard. In prophecy it denotes a solar period, ten of these going to the circle. The name Enoch may be written or transliterated INCH, and his years were 365, the number of days in the year. He was therefore a typal man and a standard in time and space. " And Enoch was not, for God took him."

Ten solar periods of 36 years is thus seen to be the full cycle of what is called " the divine year " as distinguished from the solar year of 365 common days, and the lunar year of 354 common days. Ten is a Divine Number according to all repute, so that its product from the square of the working number six, namely, 360, is significantly appropriate.

It will be observed that the number 36 goes into the " seven times " exactly 70 times, that is to say, 2,520/36 equals 70, and thus we are brought into terms of two divine numbers 7 and 10. It will be seen that the 3 and 12 are also employed in the formation or fulfilling of this period of 2,520 years. For 3 x 7 x 10 x 12 equals 2,520.

Through all these permutations the Working Number 6 passes like a thread of destiny. Thus from the Adamic Epoch (—3999 —4000) to the Nativity of Christ is a period of 3996 years, the date of the Nativity being —3, or —4. This period is seen to work out by a division of 6 to the Satanic Number 666, and by the " squaring " of 6, which is 36, it works out to the Divine Number 111, showing just one hundred and eleven solar periods from Adam to Christ. Here arises the great conflict between the Seed of the Serpent and the Seed of the Woman, according to the judgment : " I will set enmity between thy seed and her seed." And the further judgment that the " seed of the Woman shall bruise the serpent's head " brings into relief the great drama of the Redemption and the victory over Death, which is the wages of sin.

The " six days " of Formation or " making " may have been 6 days of 1,000 years each, it may have been a period of 6 times any great cycle of years, but it is known only to Him who made the world and all that therein is.

A Cryptic Saying

But this we know from Esdras, who, according to the record, fasted and prayed that he might be instructed in the knowledge of the appointed times.

" The world is divided into twelve parts, of which ten parts are gone already and the half of a tenth part, and there remaineth that which is over after the half of the tenth part."

Here it is necessary to bring into notice the

Great Year of Plato, which is the full cycle of the precession of the equinoxes, and which extends over a period of 25,920 years. This gives a mean annual precession of 50″. Formerly it was less than this, as is well established by astronomical calculations, but now it is more than 50″ by as much as a quarter of a second per year. This variation arises from the eccentricity of the solar orbit, similar to that which affects the motions of all the planets.

The ancients divided the whole period into Four Ages each of 6,480 years, which they called respectively the Gold, Silver, Copper and Iron Ages, terms which are repeated in the prophecies of Daniel, in relation to four successive World Powers which he saw to have their rise and fall, concerning which more will be said later. Applying this period to the text of Esdras :

The twelfth division of 25,920 is 2,160 years.

Ten parts will therefore be 21,600 years.

A tenth part is 2,592 years.

Half of a tenth part is 1,296.

Making the total years expired 22,896

Leaving unexpired at date 3,024 years.

This is exactly 84 solar periods of 36 years each, and is a complete planetary cycle inasmuch as it is the multiple of the seven planets into the twelve signs.

It gives us the date of the prophecy as —550 which is 33 years after the burning of the Temple. Esdras mentions that his prophetic work began thirty years after the burning, and this revelation appears to have had place in the third year of his illumination. Thus, if we add 6480 years (an Age) to the Adamic Epoch —3999 (—4000) we derive the End of the Age in A.D. 2481. Then from the unexpired part of the Great Year, 3024, take 2,481 and we get the date —543. But there is good reason to think that the epoch employed was —4007 (—4006 astronomical) and that it included the seven formative days. In such case the date of the prophecy would be —550, as will hereafter be shown.

This therefore is our first prophetic Key, a solar period of 36 years for each of the twelve signs, making 432 years, multiplied by the number of the planets or shemayim, which makes 432 x 7 or 3,024 years, which is the period un-expired at the time of the prophecy.

It will now be of interest to see the working out of this Law of Cycles in the historical succes-sion of events, for the purpose of which we have to assume that the " seven days " began in the year —4006.

END OF THE AGE

FROM what has been said it will be seen that the Age in which the world is now living extends from either —4007 to —4000 to either A.D. 2474 or 2481, according as we include or omit the the Formative Days prior to the Adamic Epoch. Interpreters of the prophetic records do not however attempt to define further than the 6,000 years, followed by the Millennial period of 1,000 years, after which as is stated, the forces of Evil will again be let loose for " a little while " prior to the consummation of the Age and the restitution of the Kingdom to the Father that " God may be all in all."

If, therefore, we confine our enquiry to the point of determining the 6,000 years, we shall conclude that this point is reached in either A.D. 1994 or 2001, the former being counted from the Cosmic Epoch, the latter from the Adamic Epoch. These are in common notation —4007 and —4000 respectively, but in astronomical terms they are stated as —4006 and —3999. Within the precise lines laid down by Esdras, the Hebrews have divided the Age into Seven days, each of 1,000 years, in accord with the statement : " A thousand years are as one day with the Lord," and the first six thousand years are therefore the working days of the week, the seventh being the Millennium or Sabbath.

CHAPTER III

THE GREAT YEAR

ALTHOUGH it has been determined by astronomical calculations that the period of precession answers to the latter-day revelation of the Great Pyramid, and thereby establishes a law of numerical ratios as between the year-circle and the precessional period of 25,827 years, we have to remember that we are dealing only with one quadrant of the precessional circle and a period of 6,480 years, and that this quadrant represents that segment of an ellipse in which the sun is approaching its greatest acceleration, which acceleration will continue to increase, according to our theory, until the year A.D. 2481 or thereabouts. The theory propounded is that the sun is presumed to be moving about a focal centre in an elliptical orbit, or what amounts to the same thing, an eccentric orbit that is circular, and that it follows the same law as that which determines the apparent motion of a planet in its orbit, i.e., the motion is greatest at perihelion and least at aphelion. It involves what is known as the proper motion of the sun in space, which fact incidentally destroys the theory of elliptical planetary orbits, which can only hold in relation to a stationary sun.

But however that may be, it forms no essential part of our argument. The period of 25,920 years has been given to us, and if this period is to be completed in the year A.D. 2480 then it must have had its beginning in the year —23,440, and this surely is sufficiently remote to satisfy the very oldest archæological evidences that have been produced, and incidentally to provide for that tedious process of body-building which is involved in the statement " God (the Elohim) made man out of the dust of the earth," and that later selectivity which provides for a spiritual involution at a certain stage of the process of human unfoldment, conveyed by the statement " and breathed into his nostrils the breath of lives and he became a *living soul*." The distinction between creating and making has already been notified.

THE LAW OF CYCLES

HAVING shown that the working number in the continuous formative process of human development is six, it will readily be conceived that the number 36, the square of six, and a tenth part of the divinely appointed year-circle, has a working power of great efficacy.

A division of the Great Year by 6 yields the significant period of 4320 years which is the basis of a series which together constitute the Maha-yuga or Great Age of the Hindu system, and which has undoubtedly arisen from the same source. Thus:

Kali yuga	4,320 or	120 solar periods of 36, or 6 x 6
Dvapara yuga	8,640	240
Treta yuga	12,960	360
Satya yuga	17,280	480
Mahayuga	43,200	1,200 solar peroids

The prophetic cycle of 2,520 years is 70 solar periods of 36 each. It may be brought forward in this place to show the statement of Esdras to be true, when he says : " By measure hath He measured the times and by number hath He numbered them, and He doth not stir nor move them until the said measure be fulfilled." From the Cosmogenesis in —4006 to the Exodus in —1486 is a period of 2,520 years. From the Flood to the Founding of the Kingdom of Israel —1090, is a period of 1,260 years, which is half 2,520 and an illustration of the " dividing of times." Similarly from the Call of Abraham

—1918 to the Founding of the Babylonian Empire under Nabopolasser —622, is a period of 36 × 36 years. The historical succession of Biblical events constituting vital crises and epochs in the working out of the scheme projected in the Covenant, is here set forth in further detail, showing the completion of a definite number of solar periods of 36 years, to be of the greatest significance.

THE DIVINE SCHEDULE

—4006	(7 years before Adamic Epoch) Regulation of the Cosmos.
1656	46 periods of 36
—2350	Flood Era
432	12 periods of 36
—1918	The Abrahamic Covenant. " Get thee out from among thy people."
432	12 periods of 36
—1486	The Exodus of Israel from Egypt. " Get thee out."
396	11 periods of 36
—1090	Israel becomes a Kingdom. Saul anointed by Samuel.
468	13 periods of 36
—622	Babylonian Empire founded. The first World Power.

	288	8 periods of 36
	—334	Macedonian Empire. Persia conquered by Alexander.
	360	10 periods of 36
A.D.	26	The Ministry of Christ begins
	612	17 periods of 36
	638	Omar the Saracen builds his Mosque on site of Temple.
	1260	35 periods of 36
	1898	Pogroms against the Jews. Zionist movement initiated.
	30	The fulfilling of times (—622 to —592 or 30 years)
	1928	The Year of the " Great Awakening."

In this schedule of solar cycles, there is one date which may be questioned, although its dating appears to be upheld by the exact periodicity of all others in sequence. I refer to the Flood date. This may very well have been 46 periods from the Adamic Epoch —3999, in which case it falls in the year —2343, to which it has been referred.

The depending dates, however, would seem to require the year 2350 and in such case the Patriarchal years must be reckoned from the Cosmic Epoch instead of what is called the Adamic.

The date of the Babylonian Empire and consequent oppression of Israel by that great power, is
given as —622. The Fall of the House of Judah had place in —592, after an interval of
30 years. This completed the downfall of the
Whole House of Israel, for the Ten Tribes under
Ephraim in the northern kingdom had been
exiled or taken captive by the year —719 one
hundred and twenty-seven years earlier. We are
told that the Ephraimites were led in their
exile as in triumphal marches aforetime by the
tribe of Dan, and that they settled on the banks
of Sereth (Ar-sereth, or river of Sereth) which
flows southward into the Danube (Dan-aub) and
thence into the Black Sea. The subsequent
journeying of these Ten Tribes westward across
Europe has afforded a series of landmarks and
place names, as far westward as the Marches of
Dan, i.e., Denmark whence, as we well know,
they made incursions into Britain. The dispersal
in —719, was compensated, so far as Ephraim
is concerned, by the Union of Great Britain and
Ireland, so that the British Isles came under one
flag and ensign after a lapse of exactly 2,520 years
(70 times 36) in the year 1801.

The " Indignation " began in the year —588,
four years after the Fall of Judah, and five years
before the burning of the Temple in —583. It

had a literal fulfilment in the restoration of the Temple after " seventy years," but the Shekinah, the withdrawal of which in —588 was the signal of the Indignation, was not upon it. It is held for the period of Restoration after a lapse of 70 times 36 or 2,520 years, and will be restored after the Tribulation of Jacob. From —588 the count of 2,520 years brings us to the year A.D. 1932. The word " years " used in this connection literally means a cycle or repetitive period of time, and although generally applied to a period of 365 days, the word *shanah* may mean any cycle of time, its meaning being *to repeat*. That literal years were not intended is evident from the fact that the indignation has continued with greater or less intensity until these days. But that it is not yet finally withdrawn is conveyed definitely in the words of the Lord : " Then there shall be a tribulation such as was not since the world (Age) began, nor ever shall be." This, which is prophetically known as the Tribulation of Jacob (i.e. of Israel), is definitely foretold also by Daniel, who says : " there shall be overspreading of desolations, even at the end." Specifically he dates the beginning of this tribulation as 1,290 days (years) from the Saracen invasion. " And from the time of the setting up of the abomination of desolation in the Holy Place, there shall

E

be one thousand two hundred and ninety days."
To A.D. 638 add 1290 and obtain the year A.D.
1928.

THE FOUR KINGDOMS

We have seen that there are four Ages in the
Great Year of time. Also that all dates arising
from the Cosmic Epoch —4006 will have their
sixth millennial ending in A.D. 1994, but those
that arise from the Adamic Epoch —3999 will
end their week of 6 days of 1000 years each, in
A.D. 2001.

In Daniel's interpretation of the Dream of
Nebuchadnezzar, in which a great image was set
up on the earth, having a golden head, arms and
breasts of silver, a belly of brass (*nahash*), and
limbs of iron, with feet of clay mixed with iron,
the prophet sees Four great World Powers to
rise in succession. The first of these was Babylon :
" Thou (the ruler of Babylon) art that head."
The power of Babylon passed to Persia when
Cyrus overcame Belshazzar. The power passed
from Persia to Macedonia when Alexander the
Great conquered Darius III and captured Babylon. Daniel's description of Alexander and his
campaign and the subsequent division of his
kingdom into four parts, is so exact as to have
led to the view that it must have been written

after the event. So much for the fruits of
Modernity!

The power eventually passed to Rome, the
succession being established by Augustus in
A.D. 29, and Rome continued to rule over
Palestine until the Saracen occupation in A.D.
637, a period of 666 years. Rome became established as the Holy Empire and eventually split
into two main branches, the Teutonic and the
Latin, represented by Germany and France,
appearing as the " Beast having 7 heads and 10
horns," i.e., Seven Dynasties and Ten princi-
palities. Germany and France are the two limbs
of iron in the great Image.

The " feet of clay mixed with iron " is the very
last phase of this revelation. In the " Council of
Ten " at Versailles, after the Great War, there
were men which represented Monarchies, and
men who represented Republics, i.e., iron and
clay, and these, as the prophet declared " shall
not agree together, as iron is not mixed with clay."

But it will be asked, how does it come to pass
that Daniel was able to see the rise and fall of
Four great World Powers and yet not have to
envisaged the British Empire, which is greater
than all of them put together ? The simple answer
to this question is : He did. " The Stone which
thou sawest, which was cut out without hands,

smote the image upon his feet that were of iron and clay and brake them to pieces. Then were the iron and clay, the brass and silver and gold all broken to pieces together . . . and the Stone that smote the Image became a great mountain, filling the whole earth." The intermarrying of royalty with the proletariet is foretold by Daniel: " And whereas thou sawest iron mixed with miry clay, they shall mingle themselves with the seed of men, but they shall not cleave together, even as iron is not mixed with clay." But in regard to the rise of the Fifth or Stone kingdom; the Hebrew prophet has these significant words : " And in the days of these kings," i.e., of Babylon, Persia, Greece and Rome, " shall the God of heaven set up a kingdom which shall never be destroyed; and the kingdom shall not pass to another, but shall break in pieces and consume all these kingdoms, and itself shall stand for ever."

From this we know that the Secret Builder has been at work ever since the founding of the Babylonian Empire, selecting His materials and building them into the great edifice of that kingdom on earth, over which, according to the prophecies and His own word, the Lord must shortly come to reign. " And He must reign until He hath put all His enemies under His feet. And the last enemy to be overcome is Death." Daniel knew that God would fulfil His covenant with Abraham, that his seed should be as the stars of heaven for number, that it should spread to the north, south, east and west, that it should be " a nation, and a company of nations," that no weapon formed against it should prosper, that it should possess the gates of its enemies, that its name should be called " Great " : and although the patriarch could not possibly see the fulfilment of that covenant in his own day, yet as said by the Lord at a later date : " By faith Abraham rejoiced to see my day, and was glad." We now know why the Brit-Ish people have been put through the fires of affliction, under the hammer of a hard adversity, and over the whetstone of competitive strife. It was that it should prove an effectual instrument in the hands of God in the carrying out of His great plan of human organisation and righteous government. " Israel is my Battleaxe !"

PLANETARY PERIODS

THE Seven Shemayim have already been named. The Chaldean order is primary to the scheme of cyclic manifestation. The Diurnal Order arises out of the Natural Order by reference to the 70 year cycle, and as each planet takes rule from the sun for 36 years, the whole period of manifestation is 70 x 36 or 2,520 years.

NATURAL ORDER

SATURN, Jupiter, Mars, Sun, Venus, Mercury, Moon. These planets form the annual pointers in succession and in this order, each have place in one of the signs of the zodiac according to their natural rising in the heavens, or the passage of the sun month by month throughout the year-circle.

DIURNAL ORDER

BEGINNING with the same planet, the order thus arises from the natural, as follows :

Saturday	*Saturn*, Jupiter, Mars, Sun, Venus, Mercury, Moon, Saturn, Jupiter, Mars.
Sunday	*Sun*, Venus, Mercury, Moon, Saturn, Jupiter, Mars, Sun, Venus, Mercury
Monday	*Moon*, Saturn, Jupiter, Mars, Sun, Venus, Mercury, Moon, Saturn, Jupiter.
Tuesday	*Mars*, Sun, Venus, Mercury, Moon, Saturn, Jupiter, Mars, Sun, Venus.

Wednesday *Mercury*, Moon, Saturn, Jupiter, Mars, Sun, Venus, Mercury, Moon, Saturn.

Thursday *Jupiter*, Mars, Sun, Venus, Mercury, Moon, Saturn, Jupiter, Mars, Sun.

Friday *Venus*, Mercury, Moon, Saturn, Jupiter, Mars, Sun, Venus, Mercury, Moon

and so back again to Saturday. These are the 70 cycles or solar periods, each ruling for 36 years. The first planet of each decade gives its name to the day of the week, and for this reason the cyclic order is called the Diurnal order. The planets, taken in the order of the days of the week, rule successive signs of the zodiac in the reverse order of those signs. Thus Saturn being in Capricorn, the Sun will be in Sagittarius, Moon in Scorpio, Mars in Libra, and so on round the 12 signs, until each has been allotted its ruler for the period of 36 years.

But in the Natural Order, the planets rule successive signs for one revolution or 12 years, each sign ruling for one year according to their natural succession. So that if the Sun were in Virgo, Venus would be in Libra, Mercury in Scorpio, and so on.

Joint Rulers

By this contrary revolution of the planets according to their Natural and their Diurnal orders, each sign of the zodiac is ruled jointly by two planets, and from the combined natures of these planets and their appointed offices in the world, presage is made concerning the destinies of the several countries according as they come under the rule of one or another of the Signs.

The Diurnal Ruler remains in the same sign for 36 years or one solar period. The Natural ruler remains in the same sign for 12 years. There are thus three changes of Joint Rulers in the course of a shanah or solar period of 36 years.

From these combinations all the signatures of the years arise in due succession and are accorded their appropriate names in the Book of the Torah.

Nostradamus, physician to the kings of France in his day, had an understanding of the system of Hebrew Astrology here for the first time made open like a book to the eyes of the studious, and made some remarkable predictions from this source. One is to the effect that: Le sang de juste à Londres fera faut brusler par feu de vingt et trois les six. The blood of the Just spilled in London demands its cleansing by fire in 'sixty-six. He otherwise refers to St. Paul's Cathedral as the temple of Diana, on the ancient site of which the edifice is said to stand, and seeing that the Moon in Sagittarius, the hunter's moon, is conjoined with Mars (Vulcan) he perceives its destruction by fire.

Another of his prophecies has reference to the then future greatness of the British Empire and of the decline of the then dominant Spanish power in Europe :

> Grand empire sera par l'Angleterre,
> Le pempotens plus de trois cent ans ;
> Ses copies vastes passe par mer et terre ;
> Les Lusitains ne sera pas contents.

Which may be rendered :

> Great Empire to the English arms shall be
> In fullest meed three hundred years and more;
> Her armies vast shall pass by land and sea,
> While discontented Spain is vexed and sore.

But these isolated predictions are among hundreds of others of equal merit which contributed to the fame, and subsequent fraudulent copying and misrepresentation of this great astrologer, whose prophecies, he tells us, ranged over several centuries and were for obvious reasons " joined obscurely," that is to say, without regard to their chronological sequence. They certainly covered many events of recent happening, and in connec-

tion with the Great War, there is the prophecy
that fighting would take place in all four elements
at one and the same time, namely, by submarines
and vessels on the water, by land forces, by air-
craft, and by jets de feu. Sometimes this clever
interpreter of the signs descended to particulars
of striking accuracy, and one such that recurs to
me was concerning the death of the king through
the effects of a wound in the eye received during a
tourney. The prophecy was fulfilled by Mont-
morency whose lance struck the vizier of the
king, and wounded the eye, in consequence of
which a tumour was formed on the brain which
caused the king's death, so that, " deux blesses par
une " (two wounds from one) was literally
fulfilled.

Unfortunately, however, he does not appear to
have had any clear conception of the cyclic law,
or at all events made no use of it, his predictions
ranging chiefly over the temporal changes of
various countries and, of course, largely in connection with the fortunes of France and the Roman
Church, both of which claimed his loyalty. Consequently he gives no ordered outlook upon the
future of the world as a whole or the ultimate
destiny of the nations. This is where we are able
to discern very clearly the difference between the
Science of Foreknowledge and the spiritual gift

of Prophecy, such as animated the minds of the prophets of Israel. For we are told that " Wise men of old spake as they were moved by the Holy Spirit," and it is this gift which, above all others, we are exhorted to desire : " Therefore covet spiritual gifts, but rather that ye may prophesy. For he that prophesieth speaketh unto men for edification and instruction and comfort." And truly enough, it is well to be assured that the promises of God will be fulfilled, that they are a set part in the Great Plan of human redemption and uplifting, and that they will be realised in their due season.

Modern ascriptions due to the recognition of the cyclic law are to be found in the following : the Year of Strife, 1914 ; the Year of Peace, 1918 ; the Year of Increase, 1924 ; the Year of the Red Hand, 1926 ; the year of Rising Waters, 1927; the Great Awakening, 1928. These several years were characterised by the outbreak of the Great War ; the cessation of hostilities ; the All-British Exhibition and Colonial Congress ; the Great Strike ; and the world-wide devastation by floods.

The astral pointers according to the cyclic law were : Saturn and Mars conjoined in Gemini; Venus in its own sign Libra ; Jupiter and the Sun in Aries ; Mars and Mercury in Gemini ; the

Moon eclipsed in Cancer; Saturn and the Sun in Leo—"men's hearts failing them for fear of looking at those things that are coming upon the earth." These keys are given to show that the ascriptions are not fortuitous but are directly derived from cosmic symbolism, which, as all students of astrology know, involves a knowledge of the nature and functions of the several planets, and the signs of the zodiac, together with their rulership among the nations.

Descending to particulars the exact date of the outbreak of the War was mentioned in most striking terms; the cessation of hostilities in November 1918, was predicted before the enemy had launched their final assault on 21st March of that year; the war was predicted and in print a whole year before the Chancellor of the Exchequer moved the reduction of the Army and Navy estimates; peace was predicted to take place in 1918 more than a year before the same man, then Prime Minister, sanctioned the issue of contracts for supplies for a further three years. The exact date of the Great Strike was predicted 5th May, 1926—and the date of the Great Awakening has already found publication.

These facts speak for themselves. They testify also in regard to the existence of a Law of Cyclic progress.

CHAPTER IV

THE SIGNS OF THE ZODIAC

THE Hebrew signs of the zodiac are the same in significance and order as now in use. They have undergone no change. An interpretation of their natures and potentialities, in the light of an inspired utterance, is to be found in Israel's Last Prophetic Blessing. The zodiac began then with the sign Taurus, which was the sign of the vernal equinox until the beginning of the 19th century B.C.

The order of the birth of the sons of Jacob is not that which is observed in the Prophetic Blessing, as may be seen by comparison of the two orders :

Birth—Reuben, Simeon, Levi, Judah, Dan, Naphtali, Gad, Asher, Issacher, Zebulun, Joseph, Benjamin.

Blessing—Reuben, Simeon, Levi, Judah, Zebulun, Issacher, Dan, Gad, Asher, Naphtali, Joseph, Benjamin.

The latter order is directly related to that of the signs of the zodiac beginning with Taurus.

The signs of the zodiac are called by the Hebrews " gates " of the Sun, they being the twelve gates by which the world is entered and also vacated. The Sun enters upon a new sign each month. The solar months have always been twelve in number. The Gates of the City are also twelve, three upon each side of the City. " The City lieth four-square," and the length of one side is 12,000 furlongs, and the length and the breadth and the height are all equal. Mensuration shows the cubic capacity to be 1728/8 miles, which is 6 cubed or 216, multipled by a thousand millions.

The symbolism of the heavens is elsewhere observed in the Hebrew Scriptures either in direct prophecy or as analogues. Perhaps the most striking use of the symbolism is hidden away in the prophecy of Daniel, when interpreting the dream of Nebuchadnezzar.

The Four World-Powers

Babylon is denoted by the sign Leo, which is ruled by the Sun, whose metal is Gold. The head of the Image being gold, and Bab-el-On being the " gate " or port of the Sun, it follows that Babylon is denoted as the head. Hence Daniel said : " Thou art that head." The empire did not last a hundred years, being conquered by

yrus, who by name and deed is prophesied by
saiah some two hundred years before he appeared
s the deliverer of Israel : " Cyrus, he is my
riend, and shall perform all my pleasure, even
aying to Jerusalem : ' Be thou built,' and to the
Temple : ' Let thy foundations be laid.' " This
rophecy is put in evidence in very specific
erms : " Thus saith the Lord to His anointed,
o Cyrus, whose right hand I have holden, to
subdue the nations before him : I will go before
hee and make the crooked places straight, I will
break in pieces the gates of brass, and cut in
under the bars of iron : I will give thee the
treasures of darkness and the hidden riches of
secret places, that thou mayest know that I, the
Lord, *which call thee by thy name*, am the God of
Israel. For Jacob, my servant's sake, and Israel
mine Elect, *I have even called thee by thy name*, I
have surnamed thee, though thou hast not known
me."

The Second Kingdom was Medo-Persia, which,
by the hand of Cyrus, took possession of Babylon. This kingdom is the silver portion of the
image, the breast and arms, ruled by the signs
Cancer and Gemini. Cancer ruled Media, and
Gemini Persia. This juncture of the two signs
ruling as one is repeated in the Tribal symbolism
of Israel, where it appears as " Simeon (Gemini)

and Levi (Cancer), the twins." As will be seen
from the statement already made regarding the
rulership of the planets among the primary metals,
the Moon, which rules Cancer, is related to silver,
and Mercury, which rules Gemini, is the planet
allied to quicksilver.

The Third Kingdom is that of Macedonia,
known as the Greek Empire, which under the
rulership of Alexander, seized the power of Persia.
Crossing the Hellespont in the year —334 and
capturing Babylon, the great conqueror reduced
Darius III and established his power over the
Euphrates. This Third Kingdom answers to
the sign Taurus, which is ruled by Venus, and
this in turn is the planet governing copper or
brass (*nahash*). Hence Daniel perceived the symbolism of the Image in regular zodiacal and
planetary order.

The Fourth Kingdom was the Roman Empire
related in the Dream and its interpretation to the
legs of the Image, which were of iron. It answers
to the sign Aries, which is ruled by Mars and this
planet is that which is related to the metal iron.
But the seer observed that the extremities were
part of iron and part of clay. This answers to the
succession of the signs Aries-Pisces, the former
ruled by Mars, the latter by Neptune, which is the
democratic symbol and incidentally that of con-

fusion and chaos. When the two lower elements of water and earth come together under stress they form clay. Iron and clay do not mix together, and therefore Daniel prophesied that they " shall not cleave together as iron is not mixed with clay." And here he is speaking of monarchic rule and democratic rule in connection with the ten toes of the Image. Hence the prophecy that eventually the Roman Empire would be allied to democratic Governments, and that the powers in the last stages would be represented by ten who would receive their power from either kings or republican rulers. It is suggested that the " League of Ten " which formed the primary league following the Great War, answers to this description.

As has already been shown, the breaking down of the Image by the Fifth Kingdom, which is the Stone Kingdom destined to continue forever, was effected at Waterloo so far as the one foot of the Image was concerned, and on the Rhine as regards the other foot. Thus the Four great World Powers came to an end. But during the period of their decline from —622 to A.D. 637 (1,260 years) and from A.D. 637 to 1897 (1,260 years) there has been in process of formation a Kingdom, " a stone cut out without hands that has grown to be a mountain, filling the whole earth," a people ready to the hand of the Lord

F

at such time as He shall come to claim His own, the earth that He has purchased and redeemed, by whom also He will " execute judgment upon the nations " and establish His kingdom over all the earth, for " then there shall be one language and one people, and there shall be One King over all the earth."

Thus we see that while there has been a gradual decline and degeneration of the Four Kingdoms, symbolised by the *retrograde order* of the signs Leo, Cancer, Gemini, Taurus, Aries and Pisces, there has been a synchronous progressive and upward development of that power which sprang from the root of Jesse, even from Jacob the father of Joseph, the father of Ephraim: for " thence is the Shepherd, the Stone of Israel." And this progressive symbolism, beginning in Pisces, ends with Leo, the selfsame sign from which Babylon (the Gate of the Sun) took its name and symbol. It is to that Regal sign that we now look for the manifestation of the King of kings, that Lion of the tribe of Judah, whose symbol is already embodied in the Royal Standard of Great Britain.

Thus is the Covenant with Abraham made good. British enterprise allied to an inimitable faculty for colonisation has developed a herd of young bulls (*Ephraim*) into " a nation and a company of nations " whose world-wide influence has brought about the realisation of all those blessings which were promised to the Patriarch in and through his progeny throughout the ages.

The signs and their rulers, together with their metals, are here set out for the benefit of those of my readers who have neither astronomical nor astrological knowledge :

R—SIGN—D	RULER		METAL
♌ Leo	Sun	☉	Gold
♋ Cancer	Moon	☽	Silver
♊ Gemini	Mercury	☿	Quicksilver
♉ Taurus	Venus	♀	Brass
♈ Aries	Mars	♂	Iron
♓ Pisces	Neptune	♆	Mire

R—here means *retrograde*, which infers decadence.
D—means *direct*, which infers progress.

THE FOUR CORNERS

of the earth are frequently mentioned in the Hebrew text, and always refer to what were in those ancient times the four cardinal signs, Taurus, Leo, Scorpio and Aquarius. In the prophecies, however, they have a particular adjustment in which Leo is related to the south, Aqua-

rius to the north, Scorpio to the east, and Taurus
to the west, as here shown ;

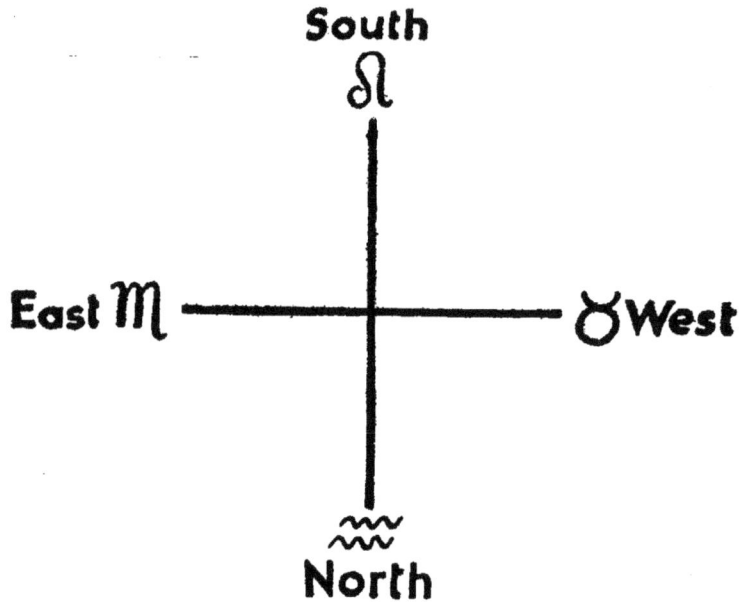

South

♌

East ♏ ———————— ┼ ———————— ♉ West

♒

North

In this remarkable glyph we have represented the
continual conflict between the north and south,
so graphically employed by Daniel in his prophecies. The kingdom of the south is that of Light,
while the kingdom of the north is that of darkness. In the south we have the symbol Leo, the
" Lion of the tribe of Judah," and against this is
set the sign Aquarius, the ruling sign of Russia,
which in the Hebrew is *Rosha*, i.e., wickedness.
The prophet Ezekiel says : The word of the Lord
came unto me saying : " Go unto the princes of

Mesech (Moscow) and Tobal (Tobolsk) and say
unto them : Thus saith the Lord, I am against
thee Prince of Rosh !" It is from the north that
the forces of anarchy and confusion are to come
" like a cloud " upon Palestine in the last of the
wars to which Israel is committed.

Moreover, this glyph embodies another great
fact of spiritual significance, which, when pro-
perly conceived by the mind, will throw a flood
of light upon some dark passages in the Hebrew
account of the anthropogenesis. We are told that
there are two great streams of life on the earth
at the present time, and that sooner or later, and
now it can only be soon than late, these two great
forces must come into final conflict. They are
specifically referred to as the Seed of the Serpent
(Scorpio-Serpentarius) and the Seed of the Woman (Taurus-Ephraim). Cain was the accursed
seed that brought jealousy, hatred, malice and
murder into the earth, the fruit of the Satanic
plot to overthrow the set plan and purpose of
Jehovah in the creation of man and the ensouling
of the Adamic race. After his condemnation and
exile he went eastward into the land of Nod and
there came into alliance with one of the serpent-
seed, whose name was Tamaiti, and named his
progeny according to the plan of his master, the
father of lies, who was " a murderer from the

beginning," by imitating the names of the Adamic offspring, even as Satan had imitated the work of Jehovah by making that travesty of the " human form divine " known to us as the anthropoid. His offspring swarms over the east, while to the west are the white men of the direct Adamic descent, mostly sons of Ephraim, i.e., Taurus, according to the glyph. We thus see how " East is east, and west is west, and never the twain shall meet " except it be in final conflict for supremacy in the earth.

THE SPHINX

is equally represented by this glyph, in that it embodies the recognised symbols of the Lion, Bull, Man and Eagle, the latter being the anti-scion of the sign Scorpio, represented in the sphere by the constellation Aquila (the eagle). It was the tribal sign of Dan, the pioneer tribe of British enterprise, and leader of the marches of Israel. The same glyph recurs in the description of the Cherubim, the wings of the Eagle over-shadowing the Altar in the Holy of Holies. It appeared as the accursed sign in the Fall, and as the Redemptive Sign on the Cross in the wilderness. In the former character it signifies spirits of iniquity and the forces of evil, or what is called by S. Paul " the mystery of iniquity " when it is said : " Behold, I have given you power to tread upon scorpions. Nevertheless rejoice not that ye have power over the spirits, but that your name is written in heaven."

The spiritual, mental, psychic and material worlds are related astrologically to the signs of fire, air, water and earth, and here appear in the form of foundation signs :

Leo	Fire	Spirit
Aquarius	Air	Mind
Scorpio	Water	Soul
Taurus	Earth	Body

These were the signs that occupied the four cardinal points at the beginning of the present age in the year —3999 (—4000) and for this reason they hold a foremost place in the symbolism of the Ancients. These four signs are those which enter into the composition of what is known as the Cosmic Cross.

The Triangle of Prophecy

MODERN theology stands helpless and mute before the wonderful revelation of the Word. It does not know the symbolism employed, and sees only a " figure of speech " where there is a definite revelation ; it does not understand the purpose of the revelation and therefore sees no plan. It has lost the power of interpretation. Hence the modern landslide in ecclesiastical affairs. While discussion rages hot and furious over the " bells and pomegranates " of the vesture, starving souls are crying out for the Bread of Life. A great effort is being made to bring about a rapprochement between religion and science. Science knows nothing of revealed knowledge and has little or no use for the inspired Word. It sees revelation only as the educated mind of man waiting upon God, where " God " means opportunity, and even commercialism.

The relation of the fiery signs (Leo, Sagittarius, Aries) to the realm of the Spirit is figured in the symbolism of the heavens where these three signs, forming the Fiery Trigon or Trinity of Flame, stand at the angles of an equilateral of 120 degrees.

In these three symbols we have depicted the threefold divine offices of the Redeemer of the World, and in them the ancient prophets beheld the whole scheme of God's purpose and the working out of His plan of salvation for the world. In the first instance we have :

Sagittarius—the Archer, with the bow of prophecy and the arrows of truth, the rider upon the White Horse, upon His head a Crown, and on His thigh a name written; and He went forth conquering and to conquer. Christ as Prophet—the fulfilling of the Law.

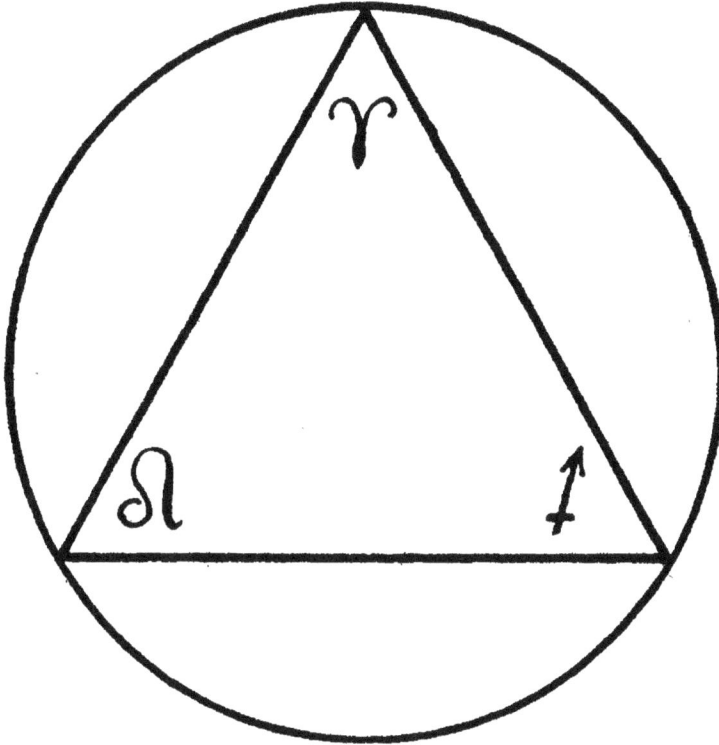

Aries—the Lamb without blemish, the firstling of the flock, an acceptable sacrifice, the peace offering. Christ as Priest—the Intercessor. " A Priest after the Order of Melchisedek."

Leo—the Lion of the tribe of Judah, the regal sign in which shines the great star Regulus. Christ as King.

In the conception of the magi who waited upon the birth of the Saviour of the World, this threefold office was specifically recognised by the presentation of appropriate gifts : gold for the king, frankincense for the priest, and myrrh for the physician or prophet. " He spake His Word and healed them."

But it will be seen, also, that these three signs have entered into the heraldry of the Stone Kingdom, that Fifth World Power to whom has been committed the custody of the Word and the fulfilling of the Covenant to Abraham, which can have none other than a material expression, in the raising up of a nation and a company of nations as effective agents of God in carrying out His purpose and plan. It is not adequate to give the Kingdom merely a spiritual significance and leave the prophecies concerning it wholly unfulfilled. Israel is a people, the kingdom is a vast organised constitution and a very material fact. It is to this prepared kingdom, which now is held by temporary custodians, that Christ will come and over which He will reign until He shall have put all His enemies under His feet. Marvel not then that the "signs" are to be seen upon the Royal Coat of Arms, as the Lion Rampant and the Unicorn with its shaft or horn. These are completed by the introduction of the sign Aries, the Lamb, and this is the ruling sign of the British people, the tribal symbol of Benjamin, " the beloved of the Lord."

There are evident signs of the leadership of the British people in the roll of the nations, inasmuch as the first four signs of the zodiac are the accredited rulers of its four corner-stones. England is ruled by Aries, Ireland by Taurus, Wales by Gemini, and Scotland by Cancer.

The sign Aries has particular significance in the production of prophetic epochs and appears to have been a landmark in the history of Israel even before its institution by Moses as the sign of the Passover (*pasach*). Abraham left Haran on the 15th day of the 7th month, in the year —1918. If we take note of the fact that the Hebrew Civil Year began in September, i.e., at the new moon nearest the autumnal equinox, which originally fell on the 24th October, —3999, then it will be seen that the 7th month answers to the new moon in Aries, the full moon of which month was consecrated to the Passover (*pasach*), when the Paschal Lamb was slain. Idolatrous Egyptians had hitherto observed the month of May (Maia) and the symbol of the Bull in connection with the beginning of the year, a pagan ritual to which Israel reverted in the absence of Moses. The great Lawgiver had not only instituted a prophetic symbolism in making the Passover coincide with the beginning of the solar year in Aries, but simultaneously effected a very important calendaric adjustment. He was " learned in all the lore and language of the Egyptians " and knew that the vernal equinox had passed from Taurus into Aries some 354 years ago at the time of the Exodus. He therefore perpetuated the landmark of astronomy by the institution of the Paschal Lamb. But not only did Moses determine the correct calendaric observance of the Passover, but in fixing upon the full moon, he was led to confirm the date of the Abrahamic Covenant, which had taken place on the 15th day of the 7th month also, and further was unconsciously confirming the prophecy that instead of Abraham's only son Isaac, " God would prepare Himself a sacrifice," which came to pass in the fulness of times at the Crucifixion. This took place on the 15th day of the 7th month also, being Friday, the 15th of Nisan, in the year A.D. 30.

It was at the Exodus, at the full moon in Aries, in the year —1486, that the Passover was instituted. It was confirmed at Gilgal forty years later, when on the 15th day of the 7th month, being the full moon in Aries, the Israelites passed over Jordan and took possession of the land of the Covenant, erecting an altar of stones, calling the name of the place Gilgal, i.e., the rolling away. This was prophetical of the " rolling away of the reproach of Israel " at Golgatha on the 15th day of the 7th month at the full moon in Aries. It will be seen therefore how sacred is this Feast of the Passover to Israel, and its modern equivalent of Good Friday to the modern representatives of these men of the Covenant, who are British, and where not British they are Christian, for the Covenant expressly extends to all of Israel, Ephraim and his companions ; to the house of Judah, and his companions.

CHAPTER V

How to Set a Horoscope

INTO the midst of much recondite matter, it seems convenient to insert something of a practical nature, and for this purpose I propose to show how a horoscope is set according to the traditional method of the Hebrews. First then, we turn to the established rulership of the planets as here shown in Pyramid Form.

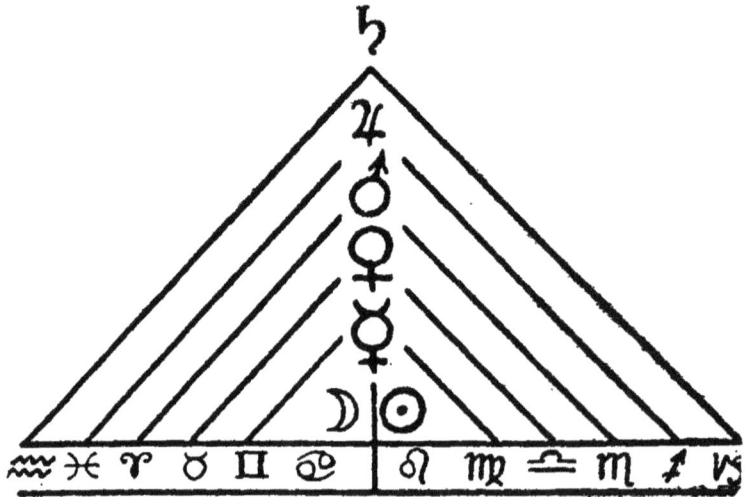

From the slope lines it will be seen that each

of the planets rules two signs of the zodiac, one of which is called the Day sign and the other the Night sign of that planet. One is male or positive in action, the other negative or female by nature. The Sun has only one sign—Leo, and the Moon only one—Cancer.

Saturn governs Aquarius and Capricorn
Jupiter rules Pisces and Sagittarius
Mars has dominion in Aries and Scorpio
Venus rules in the signs Taurus and Libra
Mercury governs Gemini and Virgo.

ACTIVE AND PASSIVE SIGNS

THESE are alternate, according to the order of the signs of the zodiac, Aries is active, Taurus passive, Gemini active, Cancer passive and so on.

CURRENT PERIOD

THE Shanah or period in which any person is born or any event of national importance may transpire, is known from the successional rule of the planets in their periods of 36 years each. Persons born after the vernal equinox of 1837 are under the primary rule of the planet Jupiter in the sign Scorpio. In the year 1873, after a period of 36 years, the signature changes, and those born after the vernal equinox of 1837 are under the primary rule of Mercury in the sign Sagittarius. After a further period of 36 years, the signature changes to Mars in Capricorn and this combination comes into play at the vernal equinox of 1909, which happened to be a new moon day and inaugurated a special chronology system during which there will be a tremendous speeding up in all departments of life and a final appeal to arms on the point of political supremacy.

From 1837 onwards to 1873, there was a great development of the sea-power of the world, and here Dan showed his ancient right of leading the tribal powers in naval armaments and equipment. In this period of Jupiter in the sign of Dan, the Danube (Dan-aub) became of paramount importance owing to the machinations of the king of the North who set over much store by Constantinople. From 1873 onwards the influence of Mercury in the sign Sagittarius awakened the echoes of an ancient prophecy: " Many shall run to and fro and knowledge shall be increased." Travelling facilities were greatly enhanced in all civilised parts of the world, and educational reforms became subject to intensive legislation. During this period also religion, so far as it was allied to the faith of our fathers, suffered a landslide. Eschatology began to show its satanic head, materialism was rife, and the established Church began to lose its grip on the minds of the people. For Mercury is in its fall in the sign Sagittarius, and the latter governs matters pertaining to prophecy and religion.

From 1909 onwards Mars in the sign Capricorn will have the inevitable effect of bringing political issues to a supreme crisis. Government will be by dictatorship and by force of arms, and constitutional methods will give place to bureaucratic regime and in some cases to that anomalistic but transient phase which can only be called republican autocracy, a form of absolutism vested in one man, in itself antetypical of the One King over all the earth.

Having determined the period in which a birth takes place, we have next to find the successional ruler of the year. For this purpose we may take an example: King George V, born 3rd June, 1865, in the second hour of the morning. This date falls between 1837 and 1873 and is therefore under the Periodical Ruler of Jupiter in Scorpio.

Starting from this signature, we count the order of the days in the week against the order of the signs:

Thursday—Jupiter in Scorpio

Friday—Venus in Libra

and so on until all the signs have been filled by their respective planetary rulers, each of which is

G

in turn dominant for 36 years, (one shanah), and
all of which change in the course of 432 years.
The count shows that the year 1865, from the
vernal equinox onwards, is ruled by the planet
Venus in the sign Pisces. This is the tribal sign
of Joseph (from thence is the Shepherd, the
Stone of Israel) to whom is adjudged many
distinctive blessings, and whose name is a symbol
of increase and expansion (Ysuph) " he shall
gather together," i.e. accumulate.

Having thus determined the ruler, i.e., the
periodic ruler dominant in that year 1865, we
now have to find the annual moderator. Starting
again from the year 1837, and the periodic ruler
Jupiter, we follow the direct order of the signs,
allotting to each sign one of the planets in the
Chaldean order, thus : Jupiter in Scorpio, Mars
in Sagittarius, Sun in Capricorn, Venus in Aquarius, and so on. It will then be found that the
annual moderator answering to the sign Pisces in
the year 1865 is Jupiter. Hence the periodic
ruler is Venus and the annual ruler is Jupiter,
and the dominant sign for the year is Pisces.
The annual rulers are dominant in their successive
signs for one year, and all are changed in the
course of twelve years, and in three cycles of
twelve, or 36 years, there is a change of period,
and 70 of these shanaim of 36 years each make one

Prophetic Age of 2520 years. Thus the cycle of time is filled.

Following the signatures for the year 1865 we have now to construct the full horoscope.

First draw a figure having twelve gates, three on the East, three on the West, three on the North, and three on the South side. These with the four corner-stones will then represent the City that " lieth foursquare."

THE TWELVE GATES

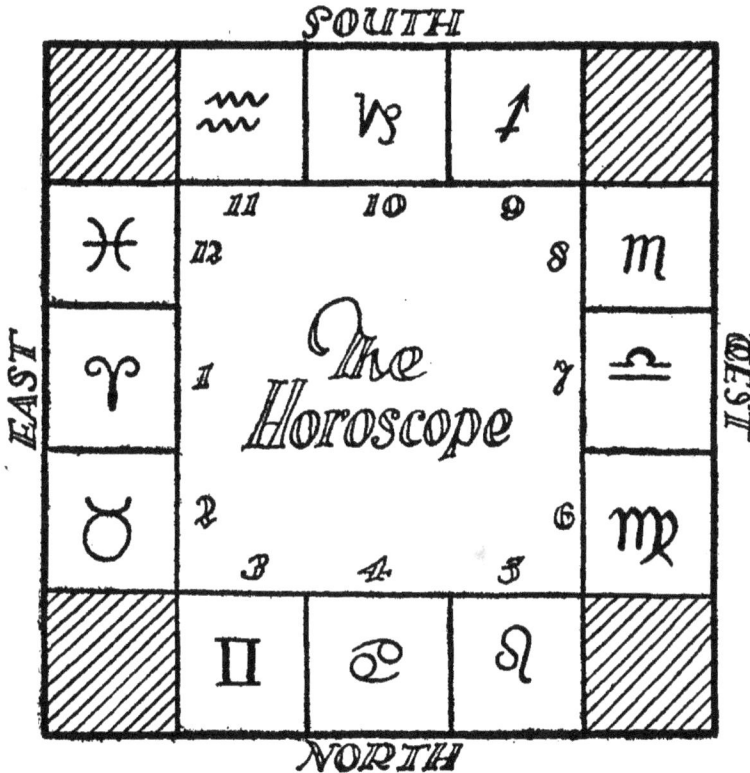

The figure as here set shows the twelve signs occupying the twelve gates at the second hour of the morning. The sun being in the sign Gemini on the 3rd June, has passed the nadir or north and is in the first section between the nadir and the Orient. Hence the sign Aries is the rising sign. This is the ruling sign of England, and the Tribal sign of Benjamin, he who " shall ravin as a wolf; in the morning he shall devour the prey and in the evening he shall divide the spoil," meaning that the early history of this tribe would be one of conquest, but its later history one of distribution. Even such has been the story of the British people under the leadership of England, for after all its conquests it has ceded powers of self-government upon its subjects, dividing the spoil to the fulfilling of the Word : " a nation and a *company of nations.*"

Benjamin means " son of my right hand." The Lawgiver being Judah, Gad, which is the fifth from Judah, is called " the right hand of the Law," and Benjamin, the fifth from Gad, is called " son of the right hand." Here again we have the sequence of the Fiery Trigon, Leo-Judah ; Gad-Sagittarius ; Benjamin-Aries.

Putting in the planets according to their respective rotational sequence in the several signs, we now have the complete

Horoscope of H.M. King George V.

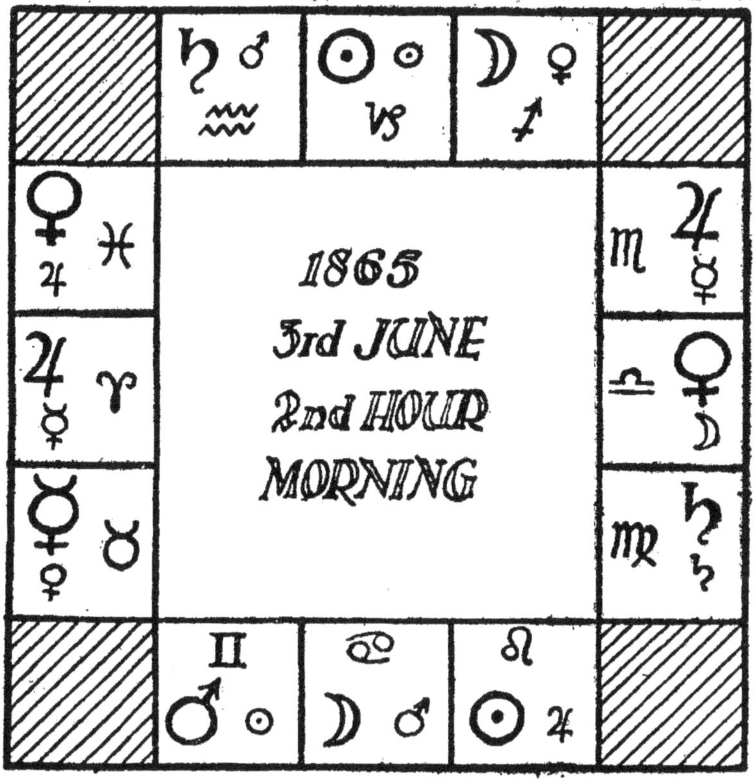
1865
3rd JUNE
2nd HOUR
MORNING

The following table of the planetary rulers, primary and secondary, for the years 1837 to 1865 will make the disposition of the factors in the example horoscope as plain as possible.

Date	♃ Scor	☽ Sagit	☉ Capr	♄ Aquar	♀ Pisc	♃ Aries	☿ Taur	♂ Gem	☽ Canc	☉ Leo	♄ Virg	♀ Libr
1837	♃	♂	☉	♀	☿	☽	♄	♃	♂	☉	♀	☿
1849	☽	♄	♃	♂	☉	♀	☿	☽	♄	♃	♂	☉
1861	♀	☿	☽	♄	♃	♂	☉	♀	☿	☽	♄	♃

EXPLANATION

FROM this table of planetary rulers it will be seen that the period which begins in 1837 is under the rule of Jupiter, which is in the sign Scorpio. Accordingly the other planets in the order of the days of the week follow the reverse order of the signs, until all the signs are fitted with their respective rulers for the whole period from 1837 to 1872 inclusive.

Jupiter also takes the first year among the secondary rulers, the signature of the first year of any period being the same as that for the period itself. Jupiter is then followed in the order of the signs by the planets in their regular Chaldean order. Thus both primary and secondary rulers are disposed among the signs of the zodiac, according to the ancient Hebrew method.

The initial year of each of the three series of twelve years, making in all thirty-six, is given for the purpose of computation. Thus for the year 1865, we start from the initial year 1861, under Jupiter and Venus in Scorpio, and proceed to 1862, Moon and Mercury in Sagittarius; 1863, Sun and Moon in Capricorn; 1864, Saturn (double) in Aquarius; 1865, Venus and Jupiter in Pisces. As this is the signature that we want, we stop here, and place these planets in that sign.

From these as starting-points we are able at once to fill in the primary and secondary rulers, according to rule already given, and thus complete the horoscope of the heavens according to the cyclic law of succession.

The horoscope as thus set is now regulated according to the hour of the birth. The month being June and the Sun in the sign Gemini in that month, this sign is placed according to the hour of birth. As this took place between midnight and two hours of the morning, the sign Gemini must hold the position of N.E. x N., and corresponds to what, in ordinary horoscopy, is called the 3rd House or division of the heavens. The other signs in their order will be disposed accordingly, and thus the whole horoscope is correctly set according to cyclic disposition of the planets at the date and time of birth.

Reference to the example horoscope of H.M. King George V. will make the above explanation as intelligible as possible to the lay reader. The symbolism of the planets and the signs of the zodiac may be found in any almanac. In the above table the signs are indicated by abbreviations of their names; their symbols do not appear. The planetary symbols however are given, without the names. The simple task of supplying the name or symbol from an almanac will afford the reader the best possible means of learning the alphabet of the heavens.

INTERPRETATION

THE rising of the sign Aries shows progressive tendencies, and the benefic configuration of the planets Jupiter and Mercury endows the mind with considerable powers of judgment and acumen. It is a sign of increase and expansion and under this auspicious signature the fortunes of Great Britain cannot be other than good.

Venus and Mercury in the sign Taurus gives stimulus to trade and financial stability, but the chief ruler being Mercury there will be a succession of very precarious phases in the fiscal affairs of the country. For Venus only rules for one year and leaves behind the influence of Mercury for many years, and neither the ubiquitous and unstable Mercury nor the sign Taurus are guarantees of stability. Hence financial affairs will not be all that could be desired and except for the dominant good influences presiding over this horoscope, there would be little sense of security assured.

Mars and the Sun in the sign Gemini is a token of strife and dissension. This division of the heavens rules over relatives, and shows treaties and agreements to be violated, with war as the inevitable consequence. It is the House of Relations, and Mars is the god of war and the creator of strife. Gemini rules Prussia, America and Wales. In all these countries there would be difficulties of relationship and many occasions for trouble. The Great War arose directly out of this configuration of Mars and the Sun in Gemini. Gemini answers to Simeon (Prussia), Cancer to Levi (Germany) and " Simeon and Levi are a twin. Instruments of cruelty (weapons of war) are in their hands." In the year 1914 the signature was Mars and Saturn in the sign Gemini, and from this configuration war was declared in the heavens and predicted for August of that year, seeing that the Sun was the ruler in Leo and was in conjunction with Mars. Leo is the ruling sign of France, the central theatre of the world strife.

The Moon with Mars, in the sign Cancer, denotes the intensive taxation of the land and properties of the country, and none less the feminist agitation which has created so many disturbances in the country. In fine, we have the disruption of the Levitical Law clearly portrayed herein, and when it is remembered that this is at the root of the British Constitution and civil law of the country, we may see that these changes are entirely subversive in tendency and effect.

The worst, however, has not yet been realised. During the course of the King's reign two great wars will have place, treaties will be formed and broken, and great changes will take place in the constitution and laws of the land.

The Sun with Jupiter in the 5th House is a most fortunate sign for the offspring of the King, and more especially for the " Prince of my people " called David, i.e., the beloved. In the regal sign Leo it is an index of supreme representation. As Princes spring from kings, so Colonies spring from parent-countries. The Brit-Ish Colonies will be the source of the greatest blessing to the throne and the " young lions " will be powerful and strong and ever ready to answer the call of the Mother-country. In this sign is the stability of the Empire assured. " The sceptre shall not depart." Saturn, doubly represented in the sign Virgo, is the planet of destruction and privation. Being in the 6th House it denotes the severe trouble that has already been experienced in connection with labour. In the wider sense it has relation to the Ottoman Empire denoted by the river Euphrates, and " the drying up of the Euphrates " has been one of the most remarkable political effects fulfilling the Word of Prophecy during the past century, and brought to its final stage by the Great War, when Turkey ceased to be a Power in Europe.

Venus and the Moon in the 7th House is a signature of much import. It denotes security in alliances, and peaceful relations with countries under the dominion of Libra, in which sign this configuration occurs, and notably Japan. This combination of influences gives happy marital relationship where the will is subservient to the behests of duty. "Issachar is an ass crouching between two burdens . . ." "He bowed his shoulders to bear." Between inclination and duty lies the priceless jewel of character.

Jupiter and Mercury in the sign Scorpio gives access to great fortune through legacies, reversions and mortgages. In the political world it favours the chance of benefits in connection with Brazil and gives promise of power in Syria.

The Moon and Venus in the sign Sagittarius denotes changes in the ecclesiastical affairs of the country, but a tendency to slackness and supineness, something of the ancient rigour of Saturn and the zeal and fire of Mars being greatly needed. It disposes however to pacific foreign relations and greatly enhances overseas trade and the prosperity of the "Dominions beyond the Seas." Pacific relations should be maintained as between Great Britain and Spain (ruled by Sagittarius), the more so as Venus, the tender twig from the royal House, has there been planted. The Sun doubly represented in the sign Capricorn (the sign of Patriarchal Descent and ancient rulership —*Malcuth*) here denotes regal security and double dominion, the indications extending to the east and west and south, but hindered and thwarted towards the north. Capricorn rules India. The position is upheld by traditional authority and respect for ancient landmarks and usages and is within the Covenant of Jacob (Capricorn) to whom the possession is given in perpetuity.

Saturn and Mars in Aquarius denotes the pouring out of the waters into the sands of the desert, false allies, bitter enmities, and severe fiscal losses due thereto. Aquarius rules Russia, and this country is destined to be a source of great loss and affliction to Great Britain by reason of its defection and most deadly treachery.

The National Exchequer is here denoted as being greatly depleted by war and by defective treaties, the effects of revolutionary movements, and repudiation of debts. This will be the occasion of a great wrestling in the Valley of Decision.

Venus and Jupiter in the sign of Piscas (Joseph) characterises the year of birth (1865) as one wholly fortunate to its scions. It here denotes "treasure laid up in store." It denotes also the making of auspicious ties and bonds. He shall walk in the paths of righteousness and his feet shall not stumble; wells of water shall spring up in the places where he treadeth, and he shall loose the bondage of his people.

In all interpretations of the chart of birth, respect must be had to the station of life into which one is born, so that if progress and success are promised as the reward of the right use of inherent faculty, it may be the more nearly defined in relation to the sphere of birth. But where birth takes place in the highest possible sphere of worldly influence, extension of this measure of power for good or evil can only overflow for the benefit or detriment of those in lowlier spheres. This was the case with David the King of Israel, who said : " Thou hast anointed my head with oil, my cup runneth over," and his excess of good fortune was shared by his people. There are degrees of fortune, and what might be accounted a good estate by one would not fill the ambitions of another. Men of need think in units, men of substance in thousands. Others do not think at all about the value of things in figures. Having enough they are content, and " a contented mind is a continual feast," or as the proverb says : " He is well paid who is well satisfied."

The Measure of Time

THE whole circle of man's life is represented by the circle of 360 degrees, which is the equivalent of 144 years, or twelve times twelve. Therefore each sign of the zodiac represents twelve years, and each two-and-a-half degrees will be represented by one year of time. Therefore by moving the Sun and planets forward by the space of two and a half degrees each year, they form new combinations by conjunction and aspect. Subsidiary to this measure, the cyclic rotation of the signs at the rate of one sign for every year, will bring other indications into effect. Thus the Sun being in Gemini with Mars is a menace of strife. After four revolutions, the Sun comes into the same sign again, and this counts to 49 years complete and 50 brings the Sun into Cancer where the Moon and Mars are stationed at the birth. Here began the Great War. The Sun rules in Gemini for one year, and finishes in Taurus after 48 years. The Sun rules in Gemini to June 1914, and then passes into Cancer, both of which signs are fraught with inimical portents involving the forces of Prussia (Gemini) and Germany (Cancer) They are twins.

It should here be noted that these measures of

time are to be applied to the correct astronomical positions of the Sun, Moon and planets, the annual motion being two degrees and a half for the primary circle which is completed in 144 years ; and monthly, two degrees and a half for the secondary circle, which is completed in twelve years.

The Hebrew method of one sign per year is based on the latter measure, and is applicable to minor changes.

CHAPTER VI

The Seven Times

WE have already seen that a "time" in pro-phetic writings is a period of 360 days or years. This may at first appear anomalous, inasmuch as the solar year is 365.25 days. But if it be noted that whatever time the sun or any other body may take to perform a circuit of the heavens it does not compass more than 360 degrees, the anomaly disappears. The simple expression of this equation is that " all concentric circles are equal," and a division of one into a definite number of parts will be a division of all others into the same number of parts of equal number of degrees. Hence the basis of time measurement is in terms of a circle of 360 degrees, which is as much as to say, the mean motion of the sun is one degree of the year-circle per day. Proceeding on this basis, it will be readily seen that " seven times " will be equal to 360 x 7 or 2,520 and it remains a question only as to why the number seven was taken to complete the cycle of times rather than any other number. This brings us

to the consideration of the septenate, which is so
strongly in evidence from the beginning to the
end of the Hebrew record. The seven days of the
cosmic work, the establishing of seven shemayim
or planetary spheres of action with their focal
centres in the planets Saturn, Jupiter, Mars,
Venus and Mercury, with the two great lights,
Sun and Moon; the Elohim or " seven spirits
before the Throne of God "; and the symbols of
these sevenfold powers throughout the religious
and civil lives of the Hebrews, clearly place this
Sacred Number in a distinctive position so far as
the Hebrew race is concerned. And when we talk
of the Hebrew race we must not forget that we are
dealing with a direct Chaldean descent, the patriarch Abraham being a descendant of Eber,
from whom they are named. It is probable therefore that the observance of the sevenfold nature of
things and the seven divisions of time by planetary shanaim or periods was traditional with them
and must have had a pre-deluvian significance.
Indeed, the Noachian account of the deluge is
prevalent in the Chaldean records with the same
observance of planetary signatures and celestial
operations. The seven " days " are thus related
to the " seven years," and these to the " seven
shanaim," and at this point, where the computation reaches to 252 years, the cycles appear to

H

end. For ten times 36 (a shanah) are 360, and seven times 360 are 2,520, so that 36 x 7 is one-tenth part of 360 x 7, and hence we get ten periods and seven periods, making 70 times 36 or 2,520, beyond which the periods of prophecy do not extend, except by repetition. The recognition of this fact leads to important conclusions, for if the consummation of any work is timed for a particular period, the event gives us some idea at least of what was aimed at, and in the prophetic sense of the Divine plan and purpose. The event, however, is most frequently of a nature which is so normally unexpected, that it leads to the idea that in the prescience of God things are foreseen and provided against. Take for instance the following terse examples :

$$
\begin{array}{ll}
\text{Cosmic Epoch} & -4006 \\
\text{Period} & \underline{2520} \\
& -1486 \quad \text{The Exodus.}
\end{array}
$$

It is only when we understand what the Exodus actually aimed at that we can apprehend the full significance of this event as a climacteric of the foundation scheme. It was not merely the liberation of the elect people, but it was also the election of a liberated people. To this event there followed the enunciation of the law, the whole of which has been incorporated in the constitution and civil law of the British people, as shown by reference to the Code of Laws of King Alfred the Great. No wonder then that this great epoch in the history of Israel is depicted in the Great Pyramid by the junction of the descending and ascending passages, called the Passover or Crossing of the Waters. From this time forth Israel was the Elect of God.

Dispersal of Israel —719
Period   2520
                A.D. 1801 The United Kingdom.

By the union of Great Britain, including Scotland, England and Wales, with Ireland in the year 1801, a further step in the consolidating of the Kingdom was effected.

Founding of Babylon —622
Period   2520
                A.D. 1898 The Great Jubilee.

In the year 1897, in the month of June, i.e., 1,897½ years from the zero of our era, and 2,520 years from the founding of the first of the Four Great World Powers foreseen by Daniel, the Great Jubilee of the Fifth Empire, i.e. the British, was celebrated on the occasion of the sixtieth year of the reign of Queen Victoria. This event was called the Diamond Jubilee, in distinction from the Jubilee of 1887. It was the celebration of the attainment of the pinnacle of true Empire, the far-flung empire " broad based upon the people's will." This in fulfilment of the prophecy " Thy name shall be called Great." So Great Britain it is to-day ; the great content of the Covenant *Brit-ain*, meaningless apart from its Hebrew origin.

Fall of Judah —592
Period   2520

          1928 The Tribulation of Jacob.

In this cycle the astral portents which attended the first event and brought about the fall of Judah under the hand of Nebuchadnezzar, are repeated. Apart from the fact that the 1290 days from Omar (A.D. 638) are now fulfilled, the cyclic conjunction of Saturn with the Sun in the sign Leo falls due in 1928 as from the vernal equinox, a combination which can only happen once in 2,520 years.

This leads to the anticipation of a further fulfilment of the prophecies that continue beyond the time of the Tribulation. As to the latter, Daniel is quite explicit and requires direct quotation in this place. He says : " And at that time (the apotheosis of the Man of Sin) shall Michael stand up, the great Prince that standeth for the children of thy (Daniel's) people ; and there shall be a time of trouble such as never was since there was a nation even to that same time " : and this prophecy is confirmed, and repeated in all essential particulars by Christ when speaking about the signs that should mark the end of the Dispensation. Here it will be noted that the Sun-ruler " Michael " is spoken of in this connection as " standing for the children of thy people." Daniel's people were men of Judah, and their children are also men of Judah, which people are ruled by the sign Leo, the dominant sign standing for the year 1928 even as in the day of Judah's former tribulation in —592. And if this expectancy is fulfilled, as doubtless it will be, we may go further and expect that the Shekinah, the glory of the Presence, will be restored in 1932, since its departure marked the Indignation to have begun, and " seven times " were to pass over Israel from that time onwards. Then we have

The Indignation   —588
Period   2520
          A.D.   1932   The Parousia.

And further we know that the period of Restoration will precede the Pleroma or Fulness of the Presence, because of the prophecy : " Verily I say unto you Elias must first come and *restore* all things." Consider for a moment the significance of this statement, following upon the question : " How then saith the prophet that Elias (Elijah) must first come ?" and the pregnant reply : " Elias has come already, and they have done unto him whatsoever they listed," with the result that they then " understood that He spake of John the Baptist." And of this John, the Lord testified : " Of those born of women, there hath not appeared a greater than he." Yet in full knowledge of the tragic death of the Baptist, it was said that " Elias must first come and restore all things." Elijah the Tishbite, John the Baptist, and Elias which is to come are one and the same Spirit. First he came to admonish Israel and caused it not to rain for three and a half years, so that a great famine fell upon the land. The sign of identity will be conspicuous in a repetition of this power, according to the prophecy : " I will give power unto my two witnesses and they shall prophesy a thousand, two hundred and three score days, clothed in sackcloth . . . these have power to shut heaven that it rain not in the days of their prophecy."

From these instances, which might be multiplied in full agreement with sacred and profane history, we see that there is a cyclic law at work, and that " by measure hath he measured the times." We may now pass to the exposition of the Shanaim or thirty-six-year periods in cyclic succession, so that what has here been said may be tested and verified.

It will be convenient to pick up the cycle of Shanaim at the year when Mars entered Gemini in the year 1657, this planet leaving that sign and going into Capricorn in 1909, after a lapse of 252 years, i.e., one-tenth of the great Ophanah of 2,520 years. The statement is that

> 10 *shanaim* equal 1 *od.*
> 7 *odim* equal 1 *ophanah,*

that is to say 10 periods of 36 are equal to " one time," and seven times are equal to one great cycle.

PLANETARY PERIODS

1657   Mars in the sign Gemini
36
1693   Moon in the sign Cancer
36
1729   Sun in the sign Leo
36
1765   Saturn in the sign Virgo
36
1801   Venus in the sign Libra
36
1837   Jupiter in the sign Scorpio

36
1873   Mercury in the sign Sagittarius
36
1909   Mars in the sign Capricorn
36
1945   Moon in the sign Aquarius
36
1981   Sun in the sign Pisces
36
2017   Saturn in the sign Aries
36
2053   Venus in the sign Taurus
36
2089   Jupiter in the sign Gemini

From this series it will be seen that after a planet, such as Mars, has continued in one sign for 432 years, it is replaced by another planet which is always the next to it in the reverse order of the spheres. Thus

Mars in Gemini	1657
	432
Jupiter in Gemini	2089
	432
Saturn in Gemini	2521
	432
Moon in Gemini	2953

Also it will be observed that any planet comes into force in another sign which is always the

eighth from the one already occupied, as Mars in
Gemini 1657, comes after a period of 252 years
or seven periods of 36, into the sign Capricorn,
which is the eighth sign from Gemini. The eighth
sign is the Reaper, and hence the sowing in
Gemini is reaped in Capricorn. The Moon in
Cancer in 1693 comes also into Aquarius in 1945.
Nevertheless Mars continues to rule in Gemini
for 432 years after 1657, and the Moon rules in
Cancer for 432 years after its entry in 1693. Hence
arise the kaleidoscopic changes that are a witness
to the unchanging law of spiritual manifestation
in the world of realities.

ANNUAL RULERS

It would be too tedious and of no real service
to the reader to set out in tabular form the
annual rulers which control the action of the
various shemayim in their respective periodic
signs. But one illustration seems to be necessary
to put the reader into touch with the scheme.

The ruler of the period is always that planet
which rules the first year of that period and it is
always followed by the planets in their direct
Chaldean order.

As there are twelve signs and only seven
planets, the annual significator is changed after
every return to the same sign. Take for example

the period of Mars in Gemini, A.D. 1657. We then have the disposition of the annual rulers as follows :

> 1657 Mars, 1658 Sun, 1659 Venus, 1660 Mercury, 1661 Moon, 1662 Saturn, 1663 Jupiter, 1664 Mars, 1665 Sun, 1666 Venus, 1667 Mercury, 1668 Moon.

This completes the circuit of the twelve signs of the zodiac, and 1669 brings Saturn into Gemini, so that each planet continues to be an annual ruler for twelve years, and is then displaced by another. Three revolutions of the heavens, at the rate of one sign per year, will complete the period of 36 years. Hence there are three series of twelve annual rulers in any period.

It is from the periodic planet, the annual ruler, and the sign in which they are conjoined for the year in question that the signature of that year has to be derived according to the principles of cosmic symbolism. For example : Mars being in the sign Gemini, it is joined in the year 1914 by Saturn, and this sign comes up in rotation for the year in question. Now Gemini is a sign of violence for it is the evil counsellor of the " Twin Sign." It is said that " instruments of cruelty " or " weapons of war " are in their hands. " In their anger they resorted to murder, and in great wrath overran the bounds." War and revolt are here portrayed. But when Mars, the god of war, is seen to hold the sign, and that Saturn, ruler of the sign Capricorn, the eighth from Gemini, is in conjunction with Mars, we know that the Reaper will take a good harvest. And if we divide the significant number 666 which stands for Sin, by 13 which stands for Death, we see that for 51.23 months Death took its toll of the fruits of sin. This may help to explain why the wages of sin is death, and why there is a set time of reckoning. In brief, all war is of evil. But yet it was possible for the God of Israel to speak of Nebuchadnezzar, the tyrant ruler and spoiler of Israel, as "Nebuchadnezzar, my servant." Truly, His ways are past finding out. Yet we are told that "Never have I set my hand to do anything but I have revealed it to my servants the prophets."

THE DIVIDING OF TIME

IMPORTANT events usually mark the midway point in any measure of time, and in the unfolding of great cycles significant historical landmarks are set up at this juncture. Thus in the " midst of the time " of the six thousand years, which are the working days of the Divine week, wherein a thousand years is as one day, we see that the midway point, three thousand years from the cosmic date 4006 B.C., and in the year —1006, the Foundations of the Temple were laid by King Solomon in Jerusalem. Seven years later, and therefore 3,000 years from the Adamic Epoch, the Temple was finished, having been " seven years in building."

Again, in the midst of the cycle of 2,520 years which separated the Founding of the Babylonian Empire by Nabopolasser —622 and the Diamond Jubilee, we strike the date A.D. 638, which we have already seen to mark the Mohammedan occupation of Palestine and the important epoch mentioned by Daniel, the setting up of the abomination that maketh desolate in the Holy Place.

Similarly there are important crises observed in the midst of any cycle, whether it be short or long. Thus in the period of Mars, the midst of the time coincided with the industrial war which centred in Great Britain and extended its ramifications to other countries. This crisis was predicted from the fact of that year 1926 coinciding with Mars and Mercury conjoined in the sign Gemini, which corresponded with the signature of the Year of the Red Hand. It was found that the greater strike was not only engineered but also financed from Russia. Mars entered upon its cycle of 36 years in 1909 under Capricorn, which is the first year of that cycle, and the sixth would fall under Gemini in the year 1914, and by the addition of a circle of twelve signs, we come to Gemini again in the year 1926. But whereas in the first case, the Great War, Saturn was with Mars in Gemini, in the latter case, 1926 strike, Mercury was with Mars. Hence the inflection of significance, Saturn being in Capricorn the political sign and ruling the eighth House which is death and destruction, while Mercury was in its own sign Gemini which has rule over means of communication, transport, railways, etc., according to the ancient canon of the Chaldeans, wherein railways had no place, but all means of communication, roadways, bridges, cavalcades, etc., were of equal importance.

Thus by all marks we are assured of the continuous working out of a set plan and purpose in the scheme of things, with the shemayim as the disposing factors as from the beginning.

CHAPTER VII

Modern Predictions

IT would not be entirely fair to conclude even a short treatise such as this without making due mention of some of the more remarkable predictions which have been inspired from this source. It goes without saying that the mere statement of a periodic conjunction of planets in any particular sign of the zodiac has no significance for the average person who may safely be said to have no knowledge whatever of cosmic symbolism. A work on this latter subject has already appeared and will repay the trouble of reading. In some books there is much more information suggested than stated, more to be read " between the lines " than in the text itself. This probably is the case with Cosmic Symbolism. But when once we are acquainted with the fact that the universe is built on order and number and that terrestrial developments follow the lines or the " pattern of things in the heavens," and that man and his greater environment are closely linked together, the whole subject of the science of foreknowledge takes on a light which throws its lustre into many dark places and unsuspected corners of human investigation and research.

It has already been shown that the signature of the year derived from the dominant rulers and zodiacal position of the seven lights according to their cyclic progress, have responded closely to the events that have characterised the year in question. But if this were the whole structure of the scheme it would indeed be simple. There are however wheels within wheels, and what applies to the world at large may not be apposite in regard to any particular territory. We have to determine first of all what countries are ruled by each of the signs, and when this is done the prognostics have to be drawn from the orientation of that particular sign. As for instance in the horoscope of China, ruled by the sign Cancer, we find that this sign comes up with an eclipsed Moon in the year 1927. Placing this sign on the ascendant for the country, the second House is ruled by the Sun and Saturn in the sign Leo, a combination which cannot work otherwise than to deplete the trade of the country and cause financial embarrassment and widespread need. Dominating the situation is the sign Aries in the Midheaven with Jupiter doubly represented therein, a sure sign that the British prestige would be upheld and that it would be employed to the benefit of ordered government in the country. But relations with India (Capricorn) would not be pacific owing to Mars and Mercury being in the western angle and many disputes would arise therefrom in connection with existing contracts and treaties. It should not, however, be thought that countries ruled by opposing signs are in continual antagonism. At the present time, for instance, the sign Aries ruling England, and Libra ruling Japan, are mutually fortified by the presence of benefic planets, Jupiter and Venus respectively, but whereas Aries is attended by a double Jupiter, the same planet ruling both its Periodic and Annual revolution, the sign Libra is vitiated by the presence of Mars with Venus, an antagonism which shows considerable unrest within the country of Japan. But whensoever the cardinal signs occupy the angles for the year, as in 1928, the affairs of Great Britain, India, China and Japan, come into prominence. The same remark applies to other countries ruled by other signs which may successively come up to the Midheaven and Ascendant, Nadir and Descendant of the horoscope for the year.

Probably the greatest event that has happened within the history of man during the present age of the world, was the Great War of 1914-18 and as it affords considerable scope for purposes of illustration it may be recalled in this place. In the first instance it will be noted that there was a conjunction of the malefic planets Saturn and Mars in the violent sign Gemini in August 1913. That year was under the rule of the sign Taurus, but the next year from March 21st onwards was under Gemini, and in this sign, the period planet was Mars, and the annual ruler Saturn. Hence the confirmation of portents which had already occurred in the heavens. There could be no doubt that this meant War, more especially when it was considered that these planets dominated the angles of the horoscope for Prussia (Gemini). So War was predicted to the date of 3rd August 1914 and found expression in print many months before it was even thought about as possible, maugre the warnings of that great patriot, F.M. Lord Roberts, so far as responsible heads of departments were concerned. April 1914 found the Chancellor of the Exchequer moving for the reduction of army and navy estimates. The Haldane report was entirely pacific. Germany was a " spiritual home." August found the world at war. Meanwhile it had been predicted that Belgium would be overrun and would suffer grievous devastations and loss of life and property " for in their anger they destroyed a wall," i.e.,

I

the buffer country of Belgium the neutrality of which had been guaranteed by the Hague Convention. But that is the Prussian way in war.

It was predicted that the War would be Titanic and would last till 1918. The astral reason for this statement was that in 1918 the signature for the year was "Peace," Venus being then ruling in the sign Libra, the Balance wherein all things come to rest.

It was predicted that Germany would at first succeed, being well served by its Navy, but that in the end the Hohenzollerns would bite the dust and gather the Dead Sea fruit of an inordinate ambition.

It was of course known that no power could stand up against the Sun (Michael) and Jupiter (Zadok) in the ruling sign of England. The destiny of the nation did not allow of such an eventuality.

But it was also seen that although Russia was an ally of France, it could not come out of the war with any measure of benefit. On the contrary it was said that it would be rent by " revolution in the midst of the war," and that the end of the House of Romanoff was involved. Here we may note that Aquarius, the ruling sign of Russia, was held by Saturn, and at first attended by Jupiter but in succession by Mars. This mixture of

" iron and lead within the urn " was a combination that could mean nothing but ruthless revolt
and the overthrow of all authority. The fruit of
that infidelity has yet not wholly matured, for
worse must happen at the appointed time. And
in regard to France, it will be observed that in
1914 the sign Leo was occupied by the Sun and
Mars. Here we get the signature of the Lion
rampant. In August 1914 there was a large
eclipse of the Sun which fell in opposition to the
place of Saturn in Aquarius 28.

This eclipse fell on the place of the great star
Regulus in the 28th degree of the sign Leo.
It was unfortunate for poor France but worse for
Russia, because it fell in opposition to the place
of Saturn in Aquarius exactly, whereas it was
not until 1916 that there was an eclipse exactly on
the place of the Sun in Leo. This eclipse, falling
on the star Regulus, the Ruler, foretold " the
breaking of sceptres and the scattering of crowns"
as a consequence of the World War, a prediction
that was seized upon by the editor of the famous
almanac of " Old Moore "* and made the subject
of a striking hieroglyphic picture. This eclipse
will reach its maximum when in conjunction with
Regulus in the year 1933 and this will be the end
of the kings of the earth, save one.

* Published by Foulsham & Co., Ltd.

Enough has been said here and elsewhere in these pages to prove, I think, that there is a veritable law of cyclic unfoldment in the course of events and that what appears to us as well within the determination and will of man is only after all a part of the great plan of human development which will eventually fulfil the Divine purpose of life. A purpose involves a plan, a plan demands its executive, and at once the whole gamut of human dependency and interplay is set in operation. As the old philosopher has said: " God does the work, men are His agents."

The basis of prophecy, therefore, rests on a recognition of this fundamental law of the correlated successiveness of events, a scheme which involves the operation of an over-ruling Intelligence, who determines the course of events towards a preconceived end. It involves more than this, however. It infers and indeed requires that the future not only exists, equally as the past, but that they are immediately related one to another by means of present action and that the future is capable of being revealed to the man of telescopic vision. This does not mean that any man is capable of " seeing " the whole of futurity. It means that he is capable of being impressed to see so much of the future as may be revealed by intelligences whose greater spiritual height gives

MODERN PREDICTIONS 133

them a wider horizon. We who search the limits
of our little life for some new thing upon its
near horizon, are impressed by the fact that although we cannot at any time see more than enters
upon our field of vision, the whole circle of things
stand in consecutive relations with one another,
and our horizon is continuous of itself. Even so
are the past, the present and the future. They
co-exist for the Mind that is high enough to
envisage them all within a single field at one and
the same instant of time. Every complete circle
of the horizon would reveal a repetition of the
same events time after time were it not for the
fact that our horizon is continually enlarging in
direct proportion to the degree of our mental
elevation. The new facts thus brought within
our ken are but extensions of the same radials
that hitherto have halted short of end upon an
all too narrow field of vision. But the world is
overcoming gravity, not by ascension of spirit,
but by acceleration of pace. Here we have the
cause of modern instability, that continual shift-
ing of the centre of action which was an abomination to the men of old. Here too we have the
immediate cause of that chaos which is bound to
overtake the reckless driver at the wheel of life.
The modern rate of speeding-up is such that a
catastrophe cannot be avoided, seeing that none

really knows whither he is going. I speak in terms of the man in the street, whose horizon is —the street.

Seeing then that the basis of Scripture prophecy is the consciousness of futurity, it remains to be seen whence this consciousness arises and how it is expressed.

" Wise men of old," it is said, " spake as they were moved by the Holy Spirit." They knew, did these old wise men, how to stand still and let the world revolve about them. They were self-contained, steadfast, and of set purpose. Like the still waters of the lake their souls mirrored the Infinite. They annihilated space and time. They lived in the Eternal Now. They heard the Voice of the Silence speaking within them, and as they heard, they wrote. " I, Daniel, heard, but understood not." Mark the perfect co-ordination of the senses which bespeaks their sanity. " The Word of the Lord came unto me, saying "—and then : " I looked and behold, I saw . . . !" It was a thousand times more important to them to listen than to speak, to hear what the Lord said than to be heard by Him. Compassed about by limitations of all kinds in that little world to which they were temporarily related by the incident of birth, they swept the infinitudes and marched across the stars. The Spirit that worketh in man doeth these things. It knows no limitations.

Herein is the distinction between the student of astral symbolism and the prophet of God. A clever artist will combine and apply his colours to produce a semblance of reality. At best he is a copyist and Nature is his tutor and also his model. And always Nature proves the better artist. So the man who by study of cosmic symbolism is enabled to make a science of prediction, is of a different vein to him who under the guidance of the Spirit speaks " as the Spirit gives him utterance," unconscious of the fact that he is employing the selfsame symbolism to loftier purpose. This has been set forth in the exposition of the prophecies of Daniel.

Science and Revelation are fundamentally one. There cannot possibly be any real conflict between true science and true religion, for one is based on empirical knowledge, the other upon revelation. The laws of the material world are a reflex of the spiritual, for matter is the ultimate expression of the spirit, as form is that of force. For every spiritual force there is a corresponding material form. The universe is the bodying-forth of the Divine Ideation. " God said, Let there be ... and there was." Study the canon of being and mark the cadenza of divine harmony.

GOD

Wisdom	Love
Truth	Charity
Intelligence	Affection
Thought	Feeling
Speech	Action

LIVING

We have no quarrel with empirical science. At all times we can call upon the experimentalist to repeat his operations and he will do it. Science *knows*. It deals with empirical and veridical facts, facts that are known from experience and facts that can be proved by experiment. But when we come into the domain of theoretical science— " science falsely so-called "—we are immediately up to our necks in a morass of speculation and doubt. And merely because our generations have been taught to accept as true that which is mere theory, the world to-day is in a state of unbelief and consequent materiality. " Seven times were determined upon Israel for her idolatry." It is a question whether we have not simply changed our idols and are as far from the knowledge of the truth as ever. It is not within the province of exact science to shape our religious beliefs or to impose its own limitations upon religion. They walk together or they walk alone, their paths are parallel and their objective one. They are both expressions of the same Spirit of Truth. But to-day we find science to be largely irreligious, and religion to be equally unscientific. The root of the evil is theoretical science, if such an anomalous term may be allowed to pass. Its speculations, which infer so much as proven facts, taking as a basis a theory that cannot be submitted to experimental proof, have led the world into a state of self-sufficiency and unbelief which is reflected in every department of human activity, and have given rise to that worst of all forms of paganism—homolatry, the worship of man. It is for him to work out his own salvation, and mighty certain is he that he can do it. Buoyed up by his mastery of some of nature's finer forces he imagines that he has only to go on and the secret of life will eventually be his. Allow that his objective is beneficent and directed to the alleviation of human suffering and need, it yet is not the way of the Spirit. Its effectiveness depends on the skill and knowledge of the mortal man. And in just that way the Science of Foreknowledge is not the same as Prophecy. Let the distinction be marked and observed. The material world of facts is a good jumping-off ground, none better, but those who

would fly must know the force of the wind even
though they cannot control it. "The wind
bloweth whithersoever it listeth and none know-
eth the way thereof." Even so is the way of the
Spirit. Daniel " found out by books the numbers
of the years." He was a student of chronological
science. But when he had got his setting and
relativity and had got to know the place of his
people in the scheme of things, then he had no
further use for books. His soul stood in the
solitudes of the Infinite, listening. " I, Daniel,
heard . . . ."

How long has it taken the scientific and the
religious worlds to discern the difference between
creation and formation. It was for the theologian
to tell the world the difference between *Bra* (He
created) and *Oshah* (He made). The hiatus that
exists between the creation of the *ath ha-shemayim*,
the elements of the planets and the earth, and the
cosmic process of forming or making the universe
from these elements, and of man from the dust
of the earth, would then have been conspicuous.
Science can have no quarrel with inspired revelation because of its terseness, and when it is said :
" God made man out of the dust of the earth,"
it is a question whether the whole process of
material evolution could be expressed in fewer or
truer words than these. But further, when it is

said that God " breathed into his nostrils the
breath of lives," science can have no question
as to the Divine origin of the human soul
unless, of course, believing as it has sometime
taught that human intelligence is a by-product
of organic chemistry, it can serve us with two
pennyworth of benevolence at the apothecary's
shop. There seems little difference between calling an atom a universe in miniature with a central
proton for sun and revolving electrons for
planets, and forthwith dissolving the said universe by electrification, and the dissolution of the
whole visible cosmos at the will of God. Yet
scientific speculation does not hesitate to say how
long this earth has existed nor how long it will
cohere. If a man can destroy an atomic universe
in an instant of time and so liberate its energy
and deploy that energy to purposes of his own,
as is automatically done in the process of living,
it seems not impossible, even from the standpoint
of speculative science, that God could make a
universe on the instant of His thought. It is not
claimed that the Hebrews have transmitted to us a
book of Science, but it is claimed that wherever
they intrude upon the domain of science they are
justified by a statement of truth. The topography,
ethnology, chronology and calendarics of the

Bible are as perfect as anything that has ever emanated from professed science.

Let the matter rest there as between theoretical science and religious orthodoxy; the hand-maidens of Truth are still Science and Revelation and together they will walk into their great inheritance.

In these pages I have set before the reader so much of the ancient science of Hebrew Astrology as is deemed expedient in a first book upon the subject, and probably I have carried the subject as far as most will care to follow it. I have often been asked by versed students of the astronomical science as to the source from which some of my vaticinations have sprung. In the present exposition the reader will doubtless find the answer to that question.

www.ingramcontent.com/pod-product-compliance
Lightning Source LLC
Chambersburg PA
CBHW062102090426
42741CB00015B/3309